MY JOURNEY, YOUR JOURNEY

MY JOURNEY, YOUR JOURNEY

The Archbishop of Canterbury, with Simon Mayo, Lord Soper, and many others, explores the Christian faith

A LION BOOK

Individual articles copyright © 1996 the authors
This edition copyright © 1996 Lion Publishing

The authors assert the moral right
to be identified as the authors of this work

Published by
Lion Publishing plc
Sandy Lane West, Oxford, England
ISBN 0 7459 3000 X
Albatross Books Pty Ltd
PO Box 320, Sutherland, NSW 2232, Australia
ISBN 0 7324 1255 2

First edition 1996
10 9 8 7 6 5 4 3 2 1 0

Acknowledgments
Front cover picture of the Archbishop by Derek Tamea

A catalogue record for this book is
available from the British Library

Printed and bound in Great Britain
by Cox & Wyman Ltd, Reading

CONTENTS

THANKS

I am most grateful to Brian Pearson upon whom the main burden of assembling and editing this collection fell, and to Val Tilley for her conscientious work in typing much of the material.

✠ George Cantuar

INTRODUCTION

Cardinal Suenons once said memorably: 'It takes many to be intelligent.' If that is true of how we learn, just think how much we owe to the friends who have shaped our lives in so many ways.

My life has been shaped more profoundly by friends than perhaps I shall ever know. In this book I want to introduce you to just a few of them. I know that some of them were very surprised to be invited to contribute. They said that they were not aware of having said or done anything that could have made the slightest impression upon me. That is understandable because, in a few cases, we have met face to face only once or twice. Others have been friends or colleagues for many years and their influence on me has been significant. However, all the people I have asked to join me in telling their story of faith have caused me to pause, reflect and review what I believe or how I express my own faith. Some have prompted me to go back to issues of doctrine and practice afresh in the light of the insight and experience they have shared. Others have caused me to reassess my motives, my actions and my attitudes.

At the beginning of each chapter I have written

an introduction to the contributor. These notes show that in spite of the variety of people whose backgrounds, insights and experiences have crossed my path, each has left a significant marker in my life. But what have these contributors in common? First, of course, all the contributors are men or women of God. They unashamedly confess the Christian faith and seek to serve Christ in what they identify as their God-given vocations. They are aware of what God would have them be and, in that knowledge, they are content even when the problems are immense and the challenges daunting.

Second, they address, in a refreshingly frank and open way, issues that many Christians either experience personally or wrestle with morally. These are, therefore, not so much stories of achievement and arrival as searching and moving on. You will not find any clanging gongs of triumphalism in these pages, though you will find expressions of confidence and assurance born of a conviction that God is in control. In some accounts you will find the doubts and dismay which preceded any thoughts or hope of resolution; you will also find some unresolved questions, though not in any sense to undermine or disable faith, but as an accepted – even welcomed – and integral part of exploration and discovery which is a feature of following the way of Christ.

I am enormously grateful to all those who have contributed to this volume. I believe the reader will be struck, as I was, by the honesty of those whose faith is undeniable but who have had to work – and go on working – at that faith. And it is because I find the Christian story so thrilling and compelling that I invite the reader to join that journey of discovery. My hope is that you will feel that this book gives you permission to talk about your doubts, fears and faith.

CAROL ANDERSON

I first met Carol when she was studying theology at St John's College, Nottingham, where I was a tutor. As one of the first women priests within the Episcopal Church of the USA, her ministry has been remarkable. Never one to shirk a challenge, Carol worked for some time in the deprived downtown parish of St Michael's and All Angels in New York.

Carol is fearless, energetic, forthright and uncompromising; and she has a real gift for teaching. In part, I am sure, this arises from her own search and a keen desire to question, and to go on questioning until answers emerge. Yet as well as her strong evangelical beliefs, Carol has a deep commitment to the church. She seeks to respect and nurture the whole personality of each individual in her care.

Listening to Carol, and watching her, right from those early days in Nottingham, has been inspiring for her enthusiasm and commitment which bring vitality to a ministry even in the toughest times and places. Carol has some important things to share with all of us and in her no-nonsense style you may find, as I have, that faith has to be worked at but both the search and the discoveries are immensely rewarding and satisfying.

'Her Story'

I grew up in a small town in New Jersey, in rural America, where just about everyone is either a member of the Church or some other volunteer organization. My parents were not members of either group, and I was not brought up in the Church. However, the effects of the Church were everywhere. The only music we had at school was the Methodist Hymnal, so I got to know every hymn Wesley ever thought of – and loved them all! I did go to Sunday School, occasionally, but only until I was seven.

When I was in High School, theological students came to the local Methodist church and one of them took a special interest in some of us. I got involved in his youth group to the extent that when I went to college, he prompted me to go to one that was loosely related to the Methodist Church. My college room-mate was the daughter of a Methodist minister, and my suite-mates went to church, so, when I had nothing else to do on Sunday, I would go to church with them. Religion courses were compulsory, so I took Old Testament and New Testament classes, not knowing much about either one of them. But I found the classes fascinating.

I started college in 1963, right in the middle of the civil rights movement and the professors in the religion department and a lot of my fellow students were getting very involved in this. Now, I came from a small town of 300 people, where nothing went on. We didn't have cars until we were seventeen, we didn't have stores, we didn't have anything. So something going on in college, along with my emerging ethical concern, was very exciting. During my first month in college, I went to be part of a major civil rights demonstration and was stunned to see police officers with guns that they were ready to use. It was more excitement than I had had in my entire life.

My involvement with civil rights began to form in me an understanding of political change and the notion that if people could get together, organize, and get political change going, the world could change. You may remember how heady the Sixties were. The demonstrations were increasing, Martin Luther King's vision of racial equality was compelling to people and I think if he had told me to go and sit on the roof for the next three years I would have done it. There was some 'rightness' about the whole thing. I was arrested several times during protests and was jailed briefly. I also became involved in the anti-war movement, protesting American involvement in Vietnam.

I majored in religion, and during my senior year in college got even more involved in working for social change. I volunteered for an exchange programme that the US Government put together to send people from northern, predominantly white colleges, to southern, predominantly black colleges. I went to South Carolina as an exchange student, for a short time. My room-mate there was a young black woman. On Easter Day, 1967, I went with her to her

Methodist church. We were followed all the way to the church by a pick-up truck with two very, very tough-looking white men in it. My room-mate was frightened beyond belief because she knew these men belonged to a sometimes violent, segregationist group called the White Citizens Council. I was very naïve, however, having grown up in a very safe environment, and just didn't believe people would do anything to hurt me.

After church we came out and were walking back to the college, when these men got out of the truck and moved towards us. My room-mate ran. I stood there like a tamed animal, not expecting anybody to hurt me. These men started yelling racial slurs and other insults at me. One of them hit me violently across the knees with a baseball bat. To this day, I can't kneel easily. I looked at the faces of the men who were doing this to me. I can still see them in my mind's eye – it was the first time in my entire life that I had seen raw evil. I realized that all the goodwill that existed in the civil rights movement, and all the political and moral change that was going on in society, could not break the back of the evil I saw. The incident didn't stop me from being involved in working for social change, but it did register in my mind, that something other than human desire, energy, or moral balance had to confront evil. Still, I had no idea what that 'something other' was.

Another college room-mate got me to attend the Episcopal church with her. I cannot tell you how boring I found it. My room-mate's solution was to take me to a 'high' Episcopal church where there were at least things to watch and smell. If it's your first time in an Episcopal church, you

14

wonder what all the people are walking up and down the aisle for. They go back one way and up the other way, and there are crosses and all kinds of things. Sometimes there's smoke and sometimes there are bells and gongs. It was a whole new church experience. I stayed with that for a while but, at the same time, I had to decide if I was going to do something academically with my interest in theology. With a religion major, one doesn't get employed very quickly! I either had to get a PhD in Theology, or I was going to go to seminary. I decided to go to seminary. One of my professors said to me that I had the ability to do the doctoral work; but I really was a 'people person', and needed to find some way to work with people on a regular basis.

I went to the Episcopal Theological School in Cambridge, Massachusetts in 1967 – the only woman in my class and the only non-Episcopalian in the entire seminary. I was still involved in the civil rights movement, very much involved in the anti-war movement and reading a lot of philosophers.

I was fascinated by philosophical ideas then, and I still am. But I found again and again that the ideas espoused did not seem to change people's lives. They would change minds and sometimes encourage commitment, but it did not go deeper than that. In everyday lives, people were getting divorced, they were having affairs, some were into drugs. People were in all sorts of trouble, but seemed to be unable to be free. As I began seminary training, I went to a Field Education Office. There you set up a weekend 'take your theology out into the parish' programme. I said to the director, 'I want to go to the toughest parish you have, because if I'm going to work in a parish I want to see the worst it can be.' Well, he sent me to work with a crusty New England rector who, when I walked in the front door for the interview said, 'I wanted a man. And I wanted a married man on top of it all.' And I said, 'Well I didn't particularly want you either!' It cleared the air and we hit it off from then on. I was there for three years. It was a wonderful time and I was confirmed alongside my junior confirmation class. I was also hooked on parish life.

When I graduated from seminary in 1970, I was unable to be ordained, as the Episcopal Church did not ordain women at that time. So I became a hospital chaplain for a year at the Massachusetts General Hospital in Boston. Once again, wanting to have the toughest assignment I could have, I asked to be the chaplain of the intensive care units and the emergency wards. There were not a lot of emergency cases coming in, but there were a lot of people having open-heart surgery, so the chaplaincy assigned me to that ward. I had been well trained in how to listen and how to get people to talk. But even though I was a chaplain, I had no sense of belief in a personal God. So, in order to be a good chaplain, I put together a prayer that I would say. It addressed God, but it could have been addressed, 'To whom it may concern'. The truth was that, even though I now had two degrees in religion, I did not know God well.

I was doing just fine until, one day, a patient who was to have triple bypass surgery asked me to come by and say a prayer with him before he went to surgery. I said I would but, quite frankly, I didn't like doing these prayers. I felt like a real fake. Hoping I would arrive too late to see Harold before he went to surgery, I walked all twelve flights of stairs to his floor. I stopped and talked to the nurses, I talked to anybody I could talk to. I had it all planned out in my mind what I would say to Harold: 'I came to see you before surgery, but you had already gone.'

Eventually, I went puffing into the room and there was Harold, prepared for surgery, sitting on the bed. He said to me, 'I knew you would come.' He was ready to go and we had just a couple of minutes. He said, 'Please pray with me.' So, I sat down next to his bed, took his hand and started my memorized prayer. But, as I started the prayer, incredible words came out of my mouth – not the prayer that I had practised. And while this powerful prayer was coming out of me, something like electricity was going through my body and out of my arm. Harold had hold of my hand and was pulling me into the bed because he wanted to pull whatever was coming out of me into him. I was flabbergasted by the whole thing. I finished the prayer and I said I hoped it would go well. Harold told me, right before I left, 'I'm going to be all right.' I said, 'I'm sure you are,' and got out of the room. I was exhausted and absolutely white as a sheet, and not from walking up the steps. I didn't know what had happened. I was so exhausted from this encounter, that I went back to the chaplain's office and slept for two hours.

That afternoon, I went back to the intensive care unit to look for Harold. He wasn't there. The operation should have taken about five hours, so I asked a nurse where he was. 'Well,' she replied, 'he hasn't come here yet.' Nor was he in the recovery unit. I thought he must have died – that was the only option. I went back to the ward and I asked the nurse, 'Has Harold died?' 'Oh no,' she said, 'the doctor wants to see you about Harold.' Now I was twenty-five years old and very unsure of myself, and when the doctor wants to see you about a patient, you know you are in deep trouble.

It turned out that the doctor was the head of the cardiology unit. I went to his office, stood there like I'd been caught stealing candy and said, 'You wanted to see me?' He asked, 'What did you do to Harold?' I said, 'I don't know. What did I do to Harold?' 'I want you to see this,' he said frantically. 'Here are the X-rays we took from the tests that we ran on him before. Here is where the by-pass needed to be done. But Harold wouldn't let us take him to surgery. He made us have an entire angiogram and kept saying, "I'm all right! I'm all right! You're not going to cut me open!" He was so frantic that we took these other tests and look, they're clear.' He looked at me and said, 'What did you do? Every time we asked Harold what happened he said, "The chaplain did it!" ' I answered with total honesty, 'I don't know.'

Harold was convinced that God had healed him and tried to talk to me about that. But, you see, the God who I believed in didn't do things like that. God was a philosophical ideal and all sorts of other things, but not personal and certainly not active in that kind of way. I buried this experience, just like I had buried the one of seeing evil, and the other about philosophical ideals not working. I buried them deep because they didn't fit in with my world view.

After my year at the hospital, I went to work as an assistant in a parish in New York City. I was ordained a deacon and became deeply involved in the movement to make it possible for women to be ordained to the priesthood. Within about two years, I single-handedly killed off the Sunday school – it dropped from two hundred kids down to about twenty-five. I was rather better at seeing people in the hospital or in counselling, that was until I started to get tired. Really tired. Because, with all my psychological and counselling training, I believed that either people had to change their own lives, or I had to change them, one or the other. One day I walked home to my apartment thinking, 'I'm not going to live to be thirty if I live this way any longer. There's got to be some way that people's lives can change without my having to do it, or their having to do it alone.'

As time went on, I began reading the New Testament a little bit more carefully. If you think the Christian faith is easy, you have not read the New Testament carefully. I began to see some of the things Jesus was talking about and I thought, 'I can't live that way. I can't forgive everybody who treats me badly. I can't give away things to the poor. I can't live with one coat.' I told myself, 'I'm going to keep struggling with this. How can I do it all?'

I continued to struggle with it until I had been ordained about six or seven years. I was not a sham, but I was living in another world, in a way. I had so many things going on in my mind. How to deal with evil? How do you deal with the fact that ideas, though they can be very powerful and very persuasive, don't always change things for the better? How do you deal with people who are in trouble, or who need love, when you have no more to give because you are so tired? And how do you deal with all those things that I knew I was supposed to deal with, and yet couldn't?

I finally realized that I couldn't last another minute as an ordained person, as a Christian or even as a human being, unless some of these problems were resolved. Evil, pain, human hurt, social disorder and brokenness, all the things we face every single day. No matter how much we might try to rise above it all and create our own future, it soon begins to fall apart because this world is a broken world and no matter how many times we try to paint it over with a rosy-coloured tint, it remains a broken world.

There is a part of me that still wants to hang onto my youthful, ideological notion that, if we can just get people to work together, then all's going to work right. But it is not so. We have a broken world. Evil happens, sickness happens, death happens, human relationships break apart. I had a heavy load by this time in my life and I had to ask the question 'Is that all there is?'

During this time, I met some people who said basically, 'None of the things you have tried in your life are working, Carol. Will you find out who Jesus is and what he has come to do?' I said, 'Wait a minute, I know all about Jesus. I have a seminary degree. I have a degree in theology – don't tell me about Jesus.' But, in truth, I really didn't know him. I knew a lot about him, but I didn't really know him: who he was and why he had come.

So I began the most incredible life change, because I began to understand who Jesus is and what he is all about. This new understanding began to answer the questions that couldn't be answered in any other way. I began to realize how Jesus dealt with evil and pain in his life and ministry, and in his death and resurrection – and I experienced radical conversion and transformation. This is the reality that I hope for others to discover and that can't happen until they understand how badly broken this world is, and that it can't be fixed by right thinking, right acting, right philosophy, right anything. There has to be some kind of supernatural action of God to turn the world around. That is what the New Testament is about – the activity of God beyond our human efforts and understanding.

I didn't become a Christian until about seven years after I was ordained. Not the best way to go about it! It has not been an easy road. If anybody tells you being a Christian is all joy, sweetness and light, they are not talking about the Christianity of the New Testament. But when you come to know Jesus Christ, the Christian faith does have the power to change your life, to re-orient you in such a way and with such a power, that you would never, ever, think of turning back. At least I know I wouldn't!

Stepping Stones to Belief

GEORGE CAREY

'Life', said a discerning person years ago, 'is understood backwards but is lived by going forwards.'

Each of us, when looking back, can see those milestones which changed our perspectives or understanding of things.

I can think of a number of stepping stones in my life that led me from a basic ignorance of the Christian faith to an acceptance that God existed. Further on I came to understand that he cared and this, in turn, brought me to a personal faith which led into a 'pilgrimage' of trust that I continue to this day.

That pattern is one which, as this book shows, is common to many believers. Common, and yet unique, for each of us is individually cherished by God and all have their own story to tell.

'I began life at a very early age,' Groucho Marx used to joke. Everyone's childhood leaves a deep impression. Mine coincided with the tension-filled lead-up to the outbreak of war, the Blitz and evacuation three times to Somerset when the war was at its most critical. My mother and father were very ordinary working-class people who came from the East End of London. I was the eldest of five children. I remember my mother as a very pretty woman whose care of her children was exemplary. She was deeply in love with her husband who was a wonderful father. We were very poor and I can remember times of real hardship, but it was the happiest of childhoods in which love, deep kindness, laughter and learning was the fabric of the Carey household. I could not have had a better start in life.

At the outbreak of war we moved to Dagenham in Essex, an enormous housing estate some twenty miles away from the East End. My parents were not academically educated people but they were deeply intelligent. I am quite convinced that had they the opportunity both of them could have gone to university. My father had a tough, enquiring mind; he was interested in politics and decided quite early on that socialism, while it had much to commend it, was not the sole answer to the human condition. He certainly did not believe that Conservatism had all the answers either but he remained a staunch working-class Tory until his death.

I have often wondered why this was so. After all, he was a victim of deep class divisions in society and he had to scramble for jobs when he was capable of much more. I believe the answer to that interesting question had to do with his great love for his country. He valued British institutions such as the monarchy and our form of democracy. He was distrustful – indeed, antagonistic – towards Communism and the red-hot socialism which sought the overthrow of cherished and tried values. I remember late in life, when he was a porter in a Dagenham hospital, a union official attempted to get the ancillary staff out on strike but Dad intervened and reminded porters, kitchen staff and others that their primary concern should be for the smooth running of the hospital so that the sick might be healed. To his satisfaction they agreed with him. My father was a tough man, combining that curious partnership of gentleness and deep personal courage.

Wartime for children was exciting, though we could hardly avoid feeling the tension and anxiety too. At night there would be the drone of aircraft, and often we would peep through the curtains to see the searchlights examining the skies. When there was a air-raid we would go down into the shelter at the bottom of the garden. But the other side of war was the stories of people killed – of friends killed and injured. Friends like Henry, a boy in my class, who never returned to school because his home was badly damaged one night and he was severely wounded.

War ended when I was just nine and life returned to normal again. We moved once more, to a larger house. From the garden we could see the square tower of Old Dagenham Parish Church in the distance. We were not churchgoers. Mum and Dad believed in God, and made sure we were all baptized – but church was remote from us. One thing that my parents were quite sure of, however, was that we were all Christians – and Church of England at that!

Adolescence is often a time of seeking and discovery. I was very happy at school. Even though I had taken the 13+ examination and passed, my parents saw no reason to disturb a happy education by sending me to the Grammar School. So I continued at Bifrons Secondary Modern School, ignorant of the fact that I would not be able to take 'O' levels there! I remember thinking very deeply about life, and only later did I discover that I was asking the philosopher Kant's three great questions: What can I know? What ought I to do? What may I hope for? In the aspirations of a teenager searching for spiritual answers, these became: Is there a God and can he be known? If there is, what difference does it make? What does the future hold?

Let me say again, I was not asking these questions because of a fundamental dissatisfaction with life. We had a secure upbringing. Despite the hardship and deep national anxiety brought about by our fight for survival, mine was a very happy childhood. Rather, it was because I had an insatiable appetite for reading, and was not easily satisfied by simplistic answers. Doubt came quickly to me then, and to this day I do not find it easy to believe anything! By that, I mean that I need to be satisfied that the answer I get is thoroughly worked out and worthy of commitment.

At the age of fifteen I had to start the search for a job. My headmaster, Mr Bass, was in no doubt that I had ability and that I would do well in some clerical profession. In most subjects at school I had been in the top five or six. I looked at several options, and at fifteen and a half became an office boy with the London Electricity Board in the East End of London. I enjoyed the job and it taught me a great deal. My thinking continued, and through my boss I was introduced to great literature. Over the next two years I fell in love with the writings of Charles Dickens and read all of them.

In the meantime, my younger brother had become a Christian. He startled me one week by inviting me to go to church with him the next Sunday. It was the church we could see from our house across the railway lines. He continued, 'You'll enjoy it. There are lots of people there our age.' So I went one Sunday. What a shock to my system! I still remember the slight feeling of terror at entering a church building and seeing the 'serious' people there. It all seemed very strange and remote that Sunday evening. Even today I am deeply convinced that few who are regular church-goers realize how forbidding church can be to those who were not brought up to attend each week.

However, I persevered, and I discovered that there were plenty of stimulating people in the church at Dagenham. People such as the twins John and David Harris, Ron Rushmer, Wendy Ryder and especially Eileen Hood – who will come into this story later. It was a lively church; a church where young people were made welcome and which held many activities for them. During the week there was a games evening; and Christian Endeavour – a discussion and worship session. Following each evening service we would go to the curate's house for coffee and 'fellowship', and to talk over the sermon.

For many people like myself, the challenge of war to faith is the feeling of waste. Why was there so much suffering and brokenness? Why was it that evil triumphed and the good, the innocent and the poor were among the very first to be its victims? The shocking revelations of the war – that over six million Jews had been slaughtered by Hitler's regime – disorientated me. Jews claimed to be the chosen people of

26

God. God did not seem to be doing a very good job in looking after his own. My journey of faith was now well on the way. I was thinking very seriously about life and about its purpose. And I was doing it along with others. Our discussions focused on the Bible and the person of Jesus Christ. As I considered him, I was drawn to this person who defied simplistic explanations. I found myself deeply puzzled by the impact he made. I did not automatically regard the New Testament as 'God-written' and infallible. I knew that the people who had written had done so to prove that Jesus was the son of God. How then could I be sure that it was an accurate story and not a piece of imaginative storytelling with little foundation in reality?

As I dug deeper into the New Testament I found that it wasn't the kind of propagandist tale of which I was suspicious. For a start, there were lots of loose ends in it; Jesus himself came across as a person who was both deeply humble, human and tender – not a God ten feet tall! And I found myself saying that, if I had been a disciple writing such a tale, I would not have been so scathing of the cowardice of the disciples who left Jesus to die all alone!

In short, the New Testament made a deep impression on me. I found it speaking to me, and it reached me in a way that no other literature did. The end of this first phase of my journey came in May 1953 when, without any fuss, and no great religious service or altar call, I became a follower of Jesus Christ and entered the kingdom of God. I don't remember making any great confession or statement of faith, but it was a simple, conscious and personal decision to follow Jesus and to model my life on his.

Since those days I have been asked many times whether I could really have made such a big decision at the tender age of seventeen. My reply has always been: Why not? By that age we are physically and mentally formed. Indeed many of our great decisions are made in our teens, including our aspirations for our life's work. So a decision of such magnitude for me was unexceptional. The acid test, of course, for such 'conversions' is what difference it makes to a person's life. For me, it was a transforming experience. I felt that God was with me, and even in me. The Bible talks of the Spirit of Jesus living within us, and that seemed to be the case. I felt a new person. I wanted to read the Bible and memorize it. But the effect of it was not to narrow my thinking. Rather it enlarged my horizons. I wanted to 'know'; I was thirsty for knowledge of all kinds. I can truly say that finding Christ meant finding education – something which has often been the case in the history of the Church.

So my first question had been answered: 'Is there a God and can he be known?' Yes, was my emphatic reply. He exists and his name is Jesus Christ.

One short year separated that marvellous encounter with the call to serve my Queen and country through National Service. During that time I continued to study the Christian faith, read books on philosophy, religion, art, poetry, history – and anything else that came my way! During that time my sisters, Ruby and Valerie, became practising Christians too, as also did my parents, much to our delight.

Some men hated their period of National Service. I didn't – I loved it. I managed to get into the Air Force and, following 'square bashing' at West Kirby, I did my training at Compton Bassett in Wiltshire to become a radio operator. Following nineteen weeks of training I found myself on a plane travelling to Egypt where I spent three months at Fayid Camp. Then, unexpectedly, I travelled to Shaibah near Basra in Iraq where I spent the final fifteen months in the RAF. Shaibah was rough and tough. There were just 120 young men there servicing a squadron of Sabre jets. I was with a team of radio 'sparks' whose job it was to man the High Frequency Direction Finding Unit. There was no chaplain and only a tiny Education Unit. The weather was very hot and for many young men there was very little to do, off-duty. That was not my problem! Two of us organized a meeting of Christians, and to our delight we found that among our colleagues there were quite a few men who were either members of churches or who were interested in finding out more. Together with the same friend I found a disused chapel on the base and opened it for worship. I conducted several services – probably very badly and quite illegally – but I am sure the Good Lord overlooked the several irregularities!

At Shaibah my second question, 'If there is a God, what difference does it make to my life?' was beginning to be answered: I began to see that as a Christian I had to live my life for God. I realized, of course, that this did not necessarily mean ordination but it certainly meant going into some work that had God's blessing and where I could serve him as a Christian.

One night I was on duty. It was the late shift which ended about midnight. The HF/DF hut was three miles from the main camp in the desert. There were no calls coming in, so I walked outside to drink in the cooler air and to see the radiance of the sky overhead. On the darkened horizon I could see the oil wells of Kuwait. 'What am I going to do after I'm demobbed?' I mused. I considered various options. I could continue with the Electricity Board but that did not appeal. I found myself asking the question: 'How may I serve God best?' The question led me to think about teaching. Yes! I would enjoy that and I felt I could make a good teacher. But what about ordination? I had never given thought to that option until then – but why not? Could that be the way God was leading me? The daunting implications of this entered my mind: I had no formal qualifications. I had to go back to school somehow!

So, demobbed, I returned home to civilian life – and to a new future. I immediately saw my vicar and he encouraged me to press towards ordination. I got down to the task of completing the necessary exams. Within eighteen months I had passed three A levels – in Maths, Economic History and English – and six O levels. It's amazing what you can do when God is at your tail! While that was going on, my relationship with Eileen Hood was deepening. Eileen lived on a local private estate and I lived on the council estate just a mile away. She is a beautiful and intelligent person, lovingly concerned for people. I was very much in love with her and so we married on 25 June 1960, halfway through my theological training and at the end of her nursing training.

All this, as they say, is history. Since then my ministry as a clergyman in the Church of England has taken me to a wide variety of situations. As a curate and vicar in Islington, theological college lecturer and principal, diocesan bishop and, over the last five years, Archbishop of Canterbury, I have come into contact with a wonderfully diverse group of people at different stages on their own spiritual journeys. Looking back over those thirty-five years I thank God for the form my life's work has taken. Together with my wife, whose contribution towards my work is immeasurable, the journey has taken me through deserts of disappointment and suffering, and also through valleys of refreshment and great challenge. We still look ahead to the future in confidence wondering what further stepping stones there will be.

Those reading this book will be at different points along their life's journey. But I want to say something to those who are wondering where their next stepping stone may be. These are things which have given confidence and encouragement to me on my journey and I want to commend them for the continuing journeys of others.

First, Christianity is a rational faith. I do not mean that we can prove the existence of God – clearly we are talking about believing something that is not as apparent as this word processor. I do mean, however, that to believe in God does not require the sacrifice of our intellect or the abandonment of thought. There are grounds for believing in a Being who created us all and whose nature is love.

In my own case, two things have been central. I think of the amazing creation of which we are but part. At one time it was usual for people to deny the existence of God, and the reasons given included that science has disproved religion. If that is so it is curious that so many scientists, including eminent people such as John Polkinghorne and

31

Arnold Wolfendale, are believers! They certainly do not see any incompatibility between worshipping a Creator and the day-by-day exploration of the wonders of the universe. What is more, the approach that said science can explain everything has come under increasing pressure from scientists themselves in recent years. Many are now talking in terms of some kind of 'external reality', even if they do not equate that with the God revealed in the person of Jesus Christ. That process will continue, and Christians can welcome and engage in such debates with confidence.

Second, God-given moral values lie at the heart of human life. It is often said that people can be moral without believing in God. That is true, they can. Indeed, many of us know people who are deeply committed to maintaining high and moral principles and committed to caring for others, yet they are not religious.

However, philosophically such a position has its own shortcomings. The philosopher Ludwig Wittgenstein started out on his philosophical career when, as a young man, he asked, 'Why should I tell the truth if I can tell a lie and get away with it?' It was a question about the basis of morality. We can push the question further. If this life is all there is and ultimately nothing is of lasting value or significance, then what really matters? But life takes on a new significance if we bring in a holy, just and loving God. Without that foundation any purely human constructs are bound, ultimately, to fail.

Third, a call to serve God. You don't have to be a clergyman to have a vocation to serve God. It is a great pity that the concept of vocation is so often missing today.

Whatever God calls us to do, or to be, matters enormously. It is a calling to serve him and our fellow human beings in every aspect of our lives. There is something deeply practical about Christianity. The office boy who, thirty-five years later, was unexpectedly chosen as Archbishop of Canterbury, was as much in a vocation then as he is now, serving a world which desperately needs God.

The first Christians were called 'people of the Way', because the Christian life was seen from the beginning as a journey, a pilgrimage and a following of One who was worthy to be followed. For me, Christianity is still a walk with God – an unfinished journey of faith and failure, of doubt and discovery, of vision and values. I am still learning. Although my growth as a Christian has included a strong intellectual strand it has never been wholly that. Christianity is a relationship with Jesus Christ who remains our contemporary. There have been times when I have wandered away from him but he has never left me. He has tracked me down and brought me home. Christianity is still for me a wonderful adventure with God which will continue until I see him face to face, when all my remaining questions will be answered.

MARTIN CAVENDER

A deep-thinking and very witty man, Martin was my legal adviser during my time as Bishop of Bath and Wells. Begowned and bewigged, standing alongside me in the sanctuary of Wells Cathedral, he looked as awesome as the Lord Chancellor. But those within view would detect a twinkle in his eye that spoke of a love of a warm-hearted and down-to-earth Christian man. Martin's style as a lawyer was, for me, a breath of fresh air. For him the law was to be a tool of the church, not a strait-jacket.

Undoubtedly Martin's training and his practice as an advocate in court equipped him to express his faith in ways that attracted, challenged and, often, entertained. He has an easy manner with all he meets. His wisdom comes not only from academic study but also from careful listening to those he encounters, helping them to give expression to things they hold dear.

When I was looking for both a competent and an inspirational director for a special evangelism project, Martin was an obvious candidate, though setting aside his legal practice was a considerable sacrifice for him, his wife Cesca and their family.

Martin tells his story with the precision and simplicity that is a mark of his trade, but equally with the conviction that speaks of how he feels God has influenced his choices and been faithful in his life.

Out of Plenty

Some years ago on the radio I heard a Jesuit priest speaking about the conversion of a celebrated French atheist. The atheist had described what had happened to him, saying, 'I do not speak of a miracle, though miracle it was. I speak of discovering in me something that had always been there.' Or perhaps he said, 'some*one who* had always been there'; the phrase passed quickly and both pictures seemed valid. Whatever it was, he was talking of a very personal experience, a personal relationship.

I have, at one time and another, been in contact with churches and people who have been convinced that there is only one formula for coming to a belief in Jesus Christ. But I am sure that, like fingerprints, there are as many ways to belief as there are people on earth. I didn't realize that until a long time after my own decision to become a Christian. I truly believed that I had been following a known way, receiving some divine tick on a check-sheet as I passed the landmarks.

I came to Christ out of plenty. I didn't *need* to turn to him, according to the world's judgment. I had everything I could possibly want. One of five brothers from a loving home, with parents who had sacrificed a great deal to provide us with an excellent education, I was happily married to Cesca; and we had three beautiful, healthy children. I was the second partner of eight in a small Somerset firm of solicitors which boasted five offices and sixty staff, based in the cathedral city of Wells with its moat and its swans and all the other trappings of the tourist brochure. We lived in a big house in a peaceful village, and everything in the garden was lovely. We had lots of real friends, were involved in the community in all sorts of 'feel good' ways, from the Church to the drama group. And yet... I was beginning to know the size of something Cardinal Newman once said: 'Fear not that your life will come to an end. Fear rather that it will never come to a beginning.'

In spiritual terms, my path had been travelled by lots before me. Baptized in the local Anglican church as a baby, I only remember being taken to church two or three times in my childhood. When I first went away to boarding school, in Taunton, I had to be helped by my new Housemaster with the standard joining question about my religious belief; 'Church of England, I suppose, Cavender?' 'Yes, sir,' said I, having no idea whether it was true, but thinking in my terror that it seemed a safe choice. It had 'England' in it, after all.

I was confirmed in the school chapel a couple of years later. Despite a painstaking and loving preparation by the school chaplain, I was not much the wiser about my supposed faith. I didn't have any great revelation or sense of being filled with the Holy Spirit when the bishop laid his hands on my head. I just hadn't been listening; or thinking very much.

Oddly, compulsory School Chapel was not the mind-numbingly boring experience I have heard other people describe, which put them off religion for life. Chapel for me was a peaceful place, with no competition. It allowed me to try out my newly-broken voice, despite the winces of the music master; and to exist for a few moments without having to prove anything to anyone. It was some years before I rediscovered that place in me, with a sense of coming home, in a little village church near Wells.

My lack of sisters, and an all-male education meant that leaving school was like coming out of a monastery. Life was fast, the colours were bright, and meeting girls turned my knees to water. Everything was flashing past me, as if the train I had been waiting to catch wasn't going to stop in the station after all; but I still had to get on board! Little things like falling in love with Cesca, qualification as a solicitor, marriage, a locum in Wells (for six months which became twenty-one years), with parties, fast cars, rugby, cricket, motor-racing, all just seemed to happen. I now thank God for the parents and brothers (and others) who held my hand through all that, in the unfolding of the Sixties.

The jigsaw of life only seems to fit as you look back at things that have happened. Why did I decide at fifteen to become a solicitor, when no one else in the family was one, and I didn't even know what a solicitor was? The school sent me to find out from the school solicitor – I came out from his office an hour later filled with goodwill but none the wiser; and terrified for some time to come that I would receive a bill for his time! Why did I go to that firm in Bath to do my articles? Why, when I was looking for interviews in London and the Midlands, where the money was, did I accept the casual suggestion that I do a six months' locum in a sleepy Somerset market town? Why, a partnership and three years later, did it seem right for someone with such a laid-back attitude to organized religion, and no formal preparation, to take over the Ecclesiastical Law speciality within the firm, and become diocesan registrar of Bath and Wells and chapter clerk to Wells Cathedral? When the shock had subsided, I told myself that it was because I fancied the wig and the gown – but now I know that even then people were praying for me and Cesca.

So went the jigsaw into place; the mystery of the choice that free will gives, revealing a pattern and design. I came into contact with people who were living a life I knew nothing about. Clergy and laypeople, they shone with a peace and security which amazed me. It was a life which seemed to have no relation to any measuring-line I had been using up to then. Cesca's parents were Methodist and had given me the first inkling of it; but now I was surrounded by other people who also shone. They spoke about the joy of prayer, and how they knew God personally through Jesus. They put their money where their mouths were, too, often giving away 25 per cent of their income when I couldn't seem to manage 10, or even 5, per cent of mine – although I knew I was earning three times what they were. In the old phrase, I knew they had something I hadn't; and I wanted it.

Cesca came to a belief in Christ about two months before I did. The children were immediately aware something had happened. So was I. Cesca had to be almost physically restrained from running down Wells High Street hugging everyone! This was new stuff, from a very private person. What Cesca didn't know was that she was using phrases which I had previously heard from others, especially my sister-in-law Catherine. Phrases like, 'I'm not afraid to die, now'; phrases which spoke of real beauty and certainty, like falling in love. This was not only new stuff; it was authentic. This experience, this decision was both deeply personal and wonderfully corporate.

The moment came one evening in December, around our supper table with some friends. I have since heard a lot of Christian friends deny having had a dramatic conversion, but I believe that is exactly what I had that evening. We sat chatting about the Royal Navy in the North Atlantic in 1943 – our friend Bob, now a senior parish priest, had been a One Badge able seaman on a Flower class Corvette, and I was fascinated. But as we spoke I was lifted out of myself, in a way both terrifying and peaceful at the same time. I had a vision of a prison cell, and I knew that all I had to do was to stand up and walk out of it. It was not an experience I have had before, or in the same way since. It was a picture of great detail unravelling in the back of my head. I believe that in that moment I saw that, despite our plenty, if I died that night I would have nothing. Cesca could not help me; this decision was mine alone. I had repented of all I had done wrong in my life; but now I needed to walk out of my strength, my self-reliance, my 'coping', if I were to walk into the fullness of life. I thank God that Bob, Jane and Cesca were there to pray for me.

Perhaps God has to use such experiences to get through to lawyers, as he did to the lawyer Saul in the Bible.

Saul was a zealous opponent of Christianity, and God blinded him temporarily as he was travelling on the road to Damascus. Finally, Saul listened to God. Certainly my defence mechanisms against God were excellent. I needed to see the evidence, to understand the whole as a matter of reasoning. Other lawyers in the Bible had had the same blocks. I was coming out of the darkness into the light; but I needed help with that last step. So God surrounded me with friends and spoke to me in a way I could not mistake (in a picture, because I am a visual person). Like the minister and hymn-writer Charles Wesley, 'my chains fell off, my heart was free; I rose, went forth and followed Thee'.

So that, I thought, was it. I had walked through a door into a very new world. There was no magical change, no puff of smoke; but I knew that I had made an irrevocable decision. But I had forgotten that it was a new 'beginning'. That suggested a continuation after the beginning, with a new shape and new colourings. This was the 'second birth' from the carol 'Hark the Herald Angels sing!' which I had sung in umpteen carol services; it meant a new learning process, a new maturing, with everything those implied. It was as if Jesus Christ now shone like an arc-lamp down the corridor of my life; but that meant that the corners and shadows were even darker and deeper than they had been before. It was no longer good enough just to scrape by morally and spiritually; I had to carry the arc-lamp down the corridor and poke it into the dark bits. This was going to be painful.

Parts of the process were more straightforward than others. At its root, the work of a solicitor is concerned with truth – I knew that I was a solicitor 'of the Supreme Court' first, and a representative of my client second. The priority was to help the court arrive at the truth; I would always do my best for my client, but I couldn't represent someone as 'not guilty' if I knew them to be guilty (a favourite dinner party question). In theory, this matched well with my clear new belief in Jesus Christ, 'the way, the truth and the life'.

Translating it into practice, especially with clients of many years, standing with whom I had grown into a particular way of doing things, was sometimes less easy. 'You were prepared to act for me in this sort of deal three years ago; what's different this time?' It became vital to be able to distinguish between truth, untruth and 'economy with the truth'. The divide between morality on the one hand and self-righteousness and piety on the other was amazingly narrow. I came across Archbishop Temple's comment: 'It's the most difficult thing in the world to be a Christian and not be priggish about it.' And my morality was not just an abstract thing; people were relying on me. The client, that I should act in his or her interests; my partners, close friends, who depended on me to pay my share of the bills by keeping the clients happy; my secretary and other staff, who needed their salaries paid; my wife and family, who relied on the income from the firm to pay for food, a roof, education and the rest. These moral questions were enormous, and answering them was now going to be a daily, hourly, constant work which had a new edge to it.

Every part of my life was up for re-assessment. What difference would all this make in the family? Should we insist on the children going to church? Should they carry on at private schools? What about private health insurance? Should I continue my involvement with the Marriage Guidance Council, not an obviously 'Christian' organization? (To that one, answer 'yes'; Marriage Guidance, now Relate, was as much of a 'good neighbour' to thousands of people in difficulty as the Good Samaritan had been.) Should I play cricket on a Sunday? What priority should I give to my church, in relation to my community? In relation to my family? Was I called (gulp) to be ordained? What did I feel about all the paraphernalia of the Church of England in relation to the freedoms of my new faith, with me a Church lawyer? A horrifying one; should I go back and make some recompense to all those people I had wronged in my life? If I should, could it be done, practically? And so on, and so on, and so forth, carrying the arc-lamp down the corridor.

I thought I had been doing things reasonably well even before we sat down to supper on that December evening, but to be a *follower* of Jesus Christ brought a different order of judgment. It was a quantum leap. It was as if I was not called to be better, but to be new; not a 'nicer person' but a true disciple.

New requirements brought new temptations. A friend wrote recently, 'personally, I have never perceived the devil as all warts and horns. I suspect he is all charm, attractive, very clever and utterly lethal; and temptations usually come in a very similar form'. So I was faced with some difficult situations.

I had been surprised by the fact that my 'conversion experience' had included a large component of emotion. As far as I could remember, no one had told me that emotional involvement was an acceptable part of religion. I had never seen a picture of Jesus laughing, or crying. Emotion was taboo; the Church was about a stiff upper lip, and reserve. But I now knew the truth was bigger than that – and it was tempting to throw out the baby of reason with the bathwater of my history, to abandon intellectual tests in favour of feelings.

Another temptation was to think that I was called to be 'religious'. I wasn't. The call of Christ was that I should be fully alive, in every possible way, in the world he had created. It was OK to laugh, to shout, to run, to go to a rock concert with my son Henry, to listen to jazz, to jump on the sofa when England beat Scotland at rugby, and the rest! In the same way, it was tempting to believe that God wanted my work; but what he really wanted was to see some fruit in my life. It was amazing, but God was more interested in what he could do *in* me than in what he could do *through* me.

It was tempting to become a 'literalist'. Fifteen years as a solicitor dealing with clients had given me enough nous not to ram my new convictions down the throats of all my friends and family, but these were certainties that could not be denied. The Bible, especially, was heady stuff. It no longer surprises me to come across clergy who were previously solicitors or barristers – the Bible has a feeling of truth about it that comes across in a way similar to a court of law. The four Gospels have the air of four witnesses in the box; telling the same story, but in subtly differing ways and language. Matthew and Luke, I found, tell the same story about twelve disciples being sent out to preach the gospel; but only Matthew, the Jew, adds the instruction 'Do not go among the

Gentiles... Go rather to the lost sheep of Israel.' Well, he would see it like that, and any experienced magistrate listening to a witness in court would instantly recognize the truth in such an offering, very different from the matching stories cooked up together by the witnesses in the car park beforehand. And the language! My late friend and Chancellor of the Diocese, George Newsom, told me that he had come to believe in Christ because the Greek used by Mark in his Gospel writing was so poor, so pedestrian, that it just had to be true. That's just the way a lawyer *would* think!

The Bible is also filled with paradoxes, a complete change from the security of the law. It describes Jesus covered with blood, sweat and spit, suffering on a foul cross like an ordinary person. The heroes of the early church were cowards who denied Jesus and hid behind locked doors for fear of the authorities. The Bible speaks of 'the service that is perfect freedom'. The more I explored, the more difficult it seemed. For example, I still don't understand the parable of the shrewd manager which is in Luke's Gospel (chapter 16); and neither does anyone I have asked. But I knew the Bible was God-breathed; I couldn't always explain or justify it, but I knew that as certainly as I knew anything. It was tremendously tempting to be a literalist – taking everything in the Bible to be literally true – as many of my new friends claimed to be, and throw out any experiences in my life which did not seem to fit in with the Bible.

In a way, I was – and am – a complex person assailed by the simplicity of the Gospel. The new temptations beckoned me down a path towards the 'holy huddle', where only the insiders fully understand the secrets of the sect, and only they can see the faith pure and true. The outcome is, of course, a critical spirit, stiff judgment of anything which does not meet The Criteria. I now understand what Jesus was saying as he stood against the hypocrisies, the legalistic attitude towards life, of the Pharisees, because I have been one of them; and, perhaps, still am. And sometimes I am like Peter, who denied Christ in his statements and actions; Pontius Pilate who saw the truth about Jesus but failed to stand up for it; Thomas who wanted to touch Jesus' wounds, to *see* the evidence, before he believed; Moses who heard God's call but wanted to find lots of reasons for not answering it. One of the revelations for me is that the Bible is not 'once upon a time'; but a record of what is happening in my daily life.

There was (and is) so much more. In particular, I shall always be grateful to the person who taught me to pray, so that prayer became as essential to my new life as breathing; and to such people as Jack Mardon and John Richardson, who threw me in at the deep end of sharing my faith with others. It was in that sharing that I discovered what it was (and who it was) that I truly believed.

The gospel is simple – overwhelmingly simple enough to satisfy the most complex of people. It contains a truth big enough to encompass the whole of every life. Above all, the gospel is people-centred, because the gospel is Jesus Christ, the Saviour who meets his people in their needs. It is personal, as that French convert I mentioned at the start had found.

I spent a short time in Zambia in missionary work, and it opened my eyes to the fact that the Zambians did not think of their Christian stories in the way I have set out my own, here. That would be just a lot of history to them. They want to know what God has been doing in my life *today*. The Zambians have got it right. The Christian life, as Cesca and I are constantly discovering, is a matter of being open to the working of the grace of God on a daily, even minute-by-minute basis. Always vulnerable, ever changing, often painful: praying continually!

I gave up my partnership as a solicitor a couple of years ago, to work full-time in evangelism and mission (as a member of the Archbishop's 'Springboard' initiative). How long this will continue is a matter for God's direction and for human judgment. Our friends who aren't Christians think it all a very odd, even irresponsible way to conduct our lives. All we can say is that we have never known the working of the grace of God in our lives as we do at the moment; and have never before known such blessings. If we are called back to the law, or on into something new, we just hope and pray that we shall hear the call clearly. And we pray for wisdom and for strength; as Paul said in his letter to the Philippians, in the Bible – strength 'to press on to take hold of that for which Christ Jesus took hold' of us.

RUTH ETCHELLS

When I was a vicar in Durham, I met a rich variety of people – and not just within the Church. I discovered in many of them a resilience and determination that matched part of my own philosophy – to say 'why not?' rather than 'why?'

Ruth, a trusted friend and mentor for over twenty years, became a highly respected member of the Church of England's General Synod, as well as principal of a leading theological college. Ruth's speeches are always well crafted, and her clarity serves as a fine model for all the speakers at Synod.

Ruth's story is a joy to read. It is one of potential fulfilled, even though the experience of her formative years might have consigned her to the back benches of professional life. Ruth knows the power of words and how much more powerful when used economically. So when it comes to theology she, more than most, knows how to interpret the truth which is found in the Bible.

For me, Ruth's journey shows the value of discipline and precision in thinking, writing and speaking – there are no short cuts. There were certainly no short cuts in Ruth's journey. Some people undervalued her, some expected – perhaps secretly

even hoped – she would fail when she took on
positions of leadership and influence. She became a
pioneer in her field and, though the pressures were
self-evident, her quiet confidence, centred on a loving
God, kept her true to herself.

On Authority in Christian Leadership

I slumped on the end of my bed, and tried not to abandon myself to tears. Though that would doubtless have relieved my feelings, I knew too well that at such a moment of exhaustion and defeatedness any good – and salutary – weep would turn into an orgy of self-indulgent wallowing. And it was nearly midnight, and I had yet another very early start tomorrow. But it had been such an awful day, such a truly awful day, that just going to bed certainly wouldn't lead to rest. I needed to focus it all to someone; Someone. Capital S. So I said it out loud to God: 'Lord, I can't do this job. I can't *do* this job...'

And the response was both immediate and comforting. In my head – or heart, I don't know which – God's response formed itself. 'Loved one,' he said, 'of course you can't. I've been waiting for you to find that out. So now you had better let me do it.' The great wave of thankfulness which swept through me then told me that this was the real thing, one of those rare but essential moments which mark turning points in our lives. With my whole heart I offered that thankfulness to God, mopped my face, got into bed and slept instantly and profoundly (for me not at all an invariable gift). And from then on, though with many mistakes and terrible slips on the way, I tackled the job I couldn't do in utter dependence on the God who could.

The job? and the moment? Near the end of my first term as principal of a university and theological college; to put it another way, a theological college and a university college, two separate entities, which were organically one whole. Two communities of able, delightful, highly individualistic persons who overlapped in their living accommodation, their committee structures, and their finances; but whose purposes were sufficiently different to make me feel like a coachman driving two teams of wholly different horses, heading powerfully and spiritedly in divergent directions.

Just to help make the situation more interesting (was it the Chinese who invented the special curse: 'may you live in interesting times'?) I was the first principal of this outfit who wasn't a priest. And, trickiest of all, I was also the first woman. (In any Church of England theological college, as it turned out: so no models available.)

Durham University is among the most northerly of English universities. St John's College with Cranmer Hall is part of the university's academic estate, but, being an independent Christian foundation, is not part of it financially. (Which meant that we were gloriously free to make policy, but rarely had the cash to carry it out properly.) Cranmer Hall, the theological college 'bit' of it, is amongst the most northerly of English theological colleges. This marked northernness, which was part of its attraction to me as a fully committed northerner myself, had made itself felt during that first term. January 1979 had the worst winter conditions we had suffered in Durham for years. On the night of my admission as principal of the college, at a most beautiful service in Durham Cathedral under whose shadow the college stands, Durham was for a time totally cut off by a snowstorm, so that people coming from even as close as Newcastle could not get through; and long-distance travellers had a very bad time of it unless, as many had, they had set out early.

That austere beginning was reinforced throughout the weeks that followed by bitter cold and snow which lasted, with intervals of relief, right through to April. Its consequences were inevitable and dire. Travel difficulties for the non-resident domestic staff meant shortage of help. Deliveries of food were intermittent and unreliable (I remember we ran seriously short of sugar). The heating broke down. Everybody – but everybody – got 'flu. The College buildings, ancient, beautiful and (then) seriously ramshackle, leaked everywhere. Our finances were rocky, and could not be spent on expensive palliatives (like the wholesale purchase and use of electric fires). Life was comfortless and frustrating. Those who have lived in communities will not be surprised to learn that fairly rapidly there developed a Sense of Ill-Usage looking for a Cause. A principal, especially a new one, is a fair target at such times.

As far as I know, no one actually blamed the cataclysmic weather on my appointment, as for instance the lightning which struck York Minster was later linked with that of David Jenkins' appointment as the Bishop of Durham. But there had been fairly considerable anxiety in some quarters about the fact that a woman was to be head of the place; for this touched the passionate conviction of some Christians who believe, based on what they understand the Bible to say, that a woman should not be in a 'headship' role. What sharpened it here was that this was a college founded by evangelical Christians, and that this particular woman would be responsible not only for the direction of the university students in John's Hall but for the training and final commending for ordination of those in Cranmer Hall training for the ministry.

So, from the first, there was an issue of 'authority': so sharp, indeed, that I was actually urged by letter publicly to resign from the appointment within days of accepting it, and well before I was due to take it up '... for the good of the college,' as it was put to me, 'which otherwise could be destroyed by your coming.' It is probably difficult now for most people, after the long-extended women's ordination debate in the Church of England and its outcome, to enter into the mindset of the late Seventies. The debate was not so open and on the move as it has been in the last five years. Certainly the vehemence and passion, both negative and positive, with which my appointment was greeted, was something I was fairly unprepared for. This was because my professional world up to then had largely not been in the Church, and gender was not a burning issue for most of us. So the propriety of the 'authority' with which I would be invested as principal had not been one of the questions for me in resolving whether to accept the job.

Yet, that night in my bedroom when I began to tackle my job in a fundamentally dependent way, I had suddenly seen Christian leadership quite differently, and with it the nature of a Christian leader's authority. I realized I had up to then, without noticing it, subconsciously accepted the leadership criteria of my culture; as indeed the Church in general seems to have done. I had looked for particular personal gifts, which could be used in God's service, as being marks of the potential Christian leader. (For some, I suppose that would have to include the gift of being of the right gender!) So, apart from the primary and all-important question of whether this was God's will for me, my chief anxieties had been whether I had the right gifts and whether they were up to the job. (I seem to remember Moses and Jeremiah, leaders in the Old Testament, struggled similarly.) And though through praying it became quite clear that God was calling me to this post (and so I was relatively unshaken by the urgings to resign from it), I still thought this was because God wanted me to use my particular mix of talents in this situation. And that these, and my actual position, blessed by God's clear calling, would supply the 'authority' I would need in leadership.

But that night I learned a much deeper truth about genuine Christian authority; that it must not be human authority which is blessed by God, but something springing entirely from God himself. It should owe nothing to the person, and everything to God. It may well call on every gift God has given us, but it is not the gifts that are our strength; indeed they can be our downfall. The miracles of Christian leadership happen when we admit that on our own we are nothing, but that God can take our weakness and turn it into strength. Ultimate Christian authority comes from being utterly dependent on God; and knowing it.

My worst mistakes, from that time on, happened when I took my eyes from that truth, seduced by this or that bit of egoism. And the best moments in all the years which were to follow happened when I was faithful to that understanding of Christian authority. So perhaps we need to go back a bit now, to what led up to that night; and forward from there to its outworkings.

I was the child of a Congregational minister, so I was familiar with the Christian faith. But I was conscious of how boringly 'good' home was, and how strict my upbringing, compared with that of most of my schoolfriends. How heroic my father had been for his faith only became fully clear to me some twenty-odd years after his death. And I was not far short of thirty before I really knew and faced the gap between the externals of Christian faith, and their inward nature. I had watched my parents exercise Christian leadership for nearly thirty years, and I had not at all begun to see into its reality.

Though there had been flashes of insight. I remember, for instance, a rare occasion of collision between my father and his congregation. We were in Liverpool, and in those days antipathies between Catholic and Protestant were acute in that city. (I don't think this incident could possibly happen there now, thanks to the marvellous work of the current Church leaders.) My father was presented with a request, at a formal church meeting, that he should preach a series of sermons against Roman Catholicism. But he refused

– he said he preached the saving love of God through Jesus Christ, and the power and wonder of that victory for the lives of all believers – including, he concluded bitingly, those of our fellow Christians, the Roman Catholics of this city.

There was dead silence. He sat down. The meeting was concluded hastily. People left silently, but stood outside in little groups talking. My father looked very lonely. (It didn't help that my mother was away.) And my teenage heart was shiningly proud of him.

Of course, I didn't know what that had cost, or how deep the rift would be, or how painfully it would be healed. I was far too naïve. But, more profoundly, nor did I know how deeply he had drawn, in that moment, on his own total dependence on God. I had seen it as a glorious struggle of will, with my father winning by the sheer force of his commitment to a 'larger truth'. That (essential) part of Christian leadership I had seen and recognized. But I had not known then that there was no glory or victory for him in that struggle, only deep agony of mind that his people should have so little understood the love he had been faithfully preaching all these years. I had not known he could only face that confrontation, with all its distresses, because he had abandoned himself to God, because he was therefore prepared to be battered and humiliated, since this was God's battle, not his, and what happened to him was immaterial. So on God he would rely; wholly.

I didn't understand any of that, and what it said about the sacrificial nature of true Christian authority. Not then or thereafter. Not until I sat on that bed that night, and learned the same truths for myself: and committed myself to living by them. And indeed in the years which followed there were for me not dissimilar lonely moments, which God, and God only, could use.

That commitment to truth whatever the cost, which was the one thing I *had* rightly recognized in my father as essential to Christian leadership, was the shining thread that led through my own journey to faith. It was where his integrity met mine: his as a minister of Christ's gospel, mine as a university student of English literature. My world of literature was a world of high feeling and arduous study, of beauty and of commitment, of grasping at the infinite yet disciplining its expression. Of uncovering the darkness of evil, of glimpsing the horrors potential in humanity, and of the powers at work beyond humanity, both evil and good. And of finding words, the right words, for all this. To my eyes his world was suffocatingly safe, petty in social patterns, kindly, uncultured, tedious, full of banal talk. There seemed nothing heroic, nothing challenging. But my father's costly commitment to truth, that I could recognize, and that I honoured.

It was after a stroke which crippled him both physically and mentally, making him as a little child, totally dependent not only on God but on those of us who loved him, that my father finally led me to God. For I had to be truthful for both of us then. Had he, all his life, been worshipping a Being who either didn't exist or who carelessly let his faithful ones needlessly suffer? Or was the God he loved, and preached with such certainty, far beyond anything I had imagined, beyond even those high visions that the finest literature invoked, countering evil far beyond the glimpses I had seen

57

in great writers? Now, more than ever, only the truth would do, whatever the cost of it. I struggled in darkness for weeks. and then one day, reading the Bible with a friend, all the petty cultural trappings fell away; I met the God my father and mother had known all the time. Met him; offered him my life; and was accepted.

I was not, I think, a natural leader; certainly not in my youth. I went steadily on with my career – teaching English, first in a grammar school, then in a college of education, then in a university. Meanwhile I was doing all I could to learn and grow in this faith that was for the first time wholly real to me. I was sophisticated in Christian vocabulary, but a little child in what that vocabulary meant. So I had to learn, learn, learn... They were marvellous years. Later I was to become an Anglican, but first I took a brief sabbatical to study for the external London degree of Bachelor of Divinity. I was an academic, so I needed to learn about my faith not only devotionally but academically as well. I had no idea how important that academic study was to be later in the future to which God was calling me.

In the meantime, life was full of interest – since my faith was about the whole of my life, it must address what I did professionally. It was clear to me that God was not calling me to ordination (somewhat to my surprise). So serving him had to be in the context of my secular teaching. Increasing responsibilities came my way – as head of an English department in a school, as a resident tutor in a college of education, as a vice-principal in a university college. Leadership, which I had never seen as a natural gift, was emerging as a consequence of following the career I was called to. Being vice-principal not only gave me an initial experience of exercising some interim authority, it also put me in a position to watch closely how final authority was exercised by the principal with whom I worked (Joan Bernard, founder principal of Trevelyan College in Durham University).

She had on her desk a small quotation, framed: 'I am among you as one who serves.' I reflected much on what that meant for the authority of Christian leadership. Serving the truth, yes. Serving not ignorantly, but as well-informed, and as thoughtfully, as one could manage, yes. But what else did 'serving' mean?

In that principal's life I saw total dedication to the task, at whatever personal cost: and unshakeable faith in God, even when distresses and tragedies could have destroyed it. 'Serving' as a Christian leader here clearly meant expending your whole life energy, if that's what it took, for the good of, for love of, this community. And it meant hanging in there with God whatever the temptation not to.

A principal in a university college in the late Sixties and through the Seventies was, in terms of 'authority', on shifting sand. What had been a hierarchical society with clearly defined rules was, by the end of the Seventies, a community governable only by consensus. Values were changing – about which there was widespread public as well as private disagreement. How to exercise the authority of leadership in such a changing moral economy was by no means clear, and was widely canvassed in debate. 'Serving' in a Christian way as a leader meant somehow holding on to integrity amidst all the shifting; but the extra expenditure of energy required in this changing world was – while stimulating! – quite costly.

When I sat on that bed that night, something of the depths of being, as a principal, among my community as 'one who serves', made itself clear to me. It meant putting off the concept of 'firstness' so often associated with leadership. Later, when it was more ordered in my mind, I talked to the gathered tutorial staff about this: that God had called me to be their leader, and that under him I would indeed lead them; but that I wanted to get rid of the notions of status that attach themselves to position, the 'firstness', and be the servant. I think that I put it badly, and that I didn't get across the glimpse I had gained. And also, of course, I didn't manage to remain completely consistent, and sometimes the vision slipped. But never completely, and never for long. For what that night had shown me was not only that I was of myself nothing, it had also shown me that the adequacy God gave was costly, for it had cost Christ his death on the cross; and that the service of Christian leadership is always a sharing of that cross. And only depending on God makes it endurable. Once you see that, then status, honour, the best seats at high tables, become pretty empty things, except as they convey love and honour from those among whom you serve. Then, they are precious as jewels. But in themselves they are nothing.

Some way on in my work at St John's College, after the usual ups and downs, I was talking with a third-year student. An able man, and a natural leader, he had earlier led a student outcry about something or other (I can't remember what) and it had all been a bit rough going; for me pretty

60

battering, for him quite triumphant. Subsequently he had stood for some public office in the university beyond the college, and been badly trounced, with the sort of humiliating invective so common to student politics.

That night, raw from the experience, he had come round to my house to mull it over. We shared its misery for a bit; then he put his hands over his eyes, fighting tears, and burst out, 'How do *you* bear it?' Out of the experience of that night sitting on the bed, and all my subsequent struggles to live by the light of what I had understood then, I answered him: by being the same person, God's person, whether the world praises you or blames you; and by knowing you have been so. By staying as close as possible to God through it all. Confessing to him when you have gone wrong, and thanking him for holding you up whatever. And by being quite sure that because you are leaning your whole weight on him you will not ultimately fall, whatever horrendous stumbles you have on the way. Of myself I am quite inadequate; and I know it.

Whatever level we lead at, we can only do right when we abandon reliance on ourselves, our natural gifts and the strategies they lead us into, and wholly rely on God. We need absolute integrity, good judgment, total commitment in love, to the community we are leading, whatever the personal cost. And it will cost not less than everything.

PETER GREEN

*I*t came as a shock when I discovered that Peter and I might never have met. His story uncovers the journey of a man who, on more than one occasion, has been close to death. For many years, Peter suffered from physical weakness due to his medical condition. But the man I grew to know and respect and whose friendship I have long valued, is, in fact, a very strong man with a resilience and will-power that leaves one very humbled and full of admiration.

Peter's strength sustained me when we worked together at St Nicholas' Church in Durham. His willingness to look at old problems from fresh angles was part of his willingness to take on new challenges and face seemingly impossible situations. His own health was but one example of his determination, his education another. Though his schooling was disrupted, he rose to a very senior level in Durham University as well as pioneering Christian Education abroad, most especially in Africa.

Peter has remained self-effacing despite his many and considerable achievements which have won him worldwide acclaim. Reflecting on Peter's journey, I have thought differently about many situations I

*would previously have found overwhelming. Peter has
shown me a God who is far bigger than all the doubts
and hesitations I can muster.*

That Work the Ides of March Begun

It was snowing heavily in Suffolk on the afternoon of Saturday, 15 March 1930 as I entered a world which was recovering from one war and anticipating the next. Economic depression was widespread. My parents, with my sister and myself, were to suffer with many others as they tried, not always successfully, to make ends meet. Times were hard, but there was an indomitable spirit in the family that was to serve us well in the troublesome years ahead. One grandfather, an authoritarian police officer; the other, a reluctant pattern-maker; a gentle, determined and astute countryman; a father who falsified his age so he could fight for his country; failure of the family business; concern about the family budget; the prediction of my early death because I was born with two teeth! The beginning is hearsay but no less influential for that. Of it I can remember nothing.

It is the same with the beginning of my spiritual life, which I can no more remember than I can remember my physical beginning. Both happened, not through my own endeavours but with the help of many other people. Like my physical beginning my spiritual start in this world had, I believe, a moment of conception, a period of gestation, a time of birth and a gradual realization of consciousness before running its course to maturity. While I am sure there are those who can recall their Christian birth, I cannot count myself among them. It used to concern me that others could say, with absolute certainty, when, how, and where they became Christians. I could not do this and sometimes I felt that I was an inferior, second-rate Christian. In moments of doubt I even wondered if I were a Christian.

One of my earliest 'religious' memories is when my maternal grandfather took me to a small Baptist church in Essex. I was about seven years old and I can still remember the sermon. I clearly recall the minister producing with one hand a maize cob from beneath his robes and, with the other hand, a maize seed. The illustration was simple, the message clear, the effect dramatic. I began thinking about the future.

My family was never very explicit in its religious expression. We never had family Bible readings; grace was never said before meals; family prayers were something I never experienced. Neither my sister nor I went to Sunday school, although on the opposite side of the road from our home there was a small Anglican mission church. Sunday evenings I used to lie in my bed in the front of our small terraced house and listen to the people singing. I learned many a hymn from those unknown worshippers some thirty years before I was to preach in their church. Although I have little recollection of religion within our family life I do remember, some years before my school days, occasionally saying bedtime prayers at home with my mother. Where, in all of this, was the moment of spiritual conception?

War was soon to bring many changes and it was only then that I was taken regularly to church, always to Evening Prayer. We went to a church where the vicar was a powerful speaker at a time when oratory was widely influential. The church was nearly always packed and the pew, just two rows in front of the tall pulpit, was indescribably uncomfortable. If I tried to look at the preacher my neck ached, if I listened to the preacher my head ached, if I tried to sit naturally my back ached: as soon as I could exercise some determination I found reasons for not going. It all meant very little to me. It was a confusing time for young and old alike.

School was not a happy experience. My scholarship to the local grammar school delighted my parents and teachers but brought me little satisfaction. Grammar school during wartime was, if anything, worse than primary school during peace time. I went through the motions, managed to keep out of trouble, and was glad when it all came to an end with an early departure into the world of commerce, which I hated. I found it all so tedious. I was so vulnerable, a strange sort of vulnerability which at the time I found difficult to comprehend. I was not in any danger from anyone except myself. I could do the meaningless work without any effort; it was simple, unrewarding in itself. Oh yes, I was rewarded with an adequate salary but, by now, I had become the sort of person who had to find the activity itself rewarding and it wasn't.

I also found it difficult to handle some of the commercial contradictions to my emerging faith. Perhaps this was caused by the inevitable immaturity through which all faith has to pass. Whatever the reason it was a very real burden as I began to question the relentless striving for the maximization of profit, the disregard of moral integrity and the dominance which the industry I worked in exercised over its consumers and its workers. The concealed, anonymous exercise of powerful commercial decisions troubled the understanding of my faith. Was capitalism, of which I was a part, nothing more than uncontrollable greed? Did it have to be? I was troubled not only by these questions but also because I seemed to be alone in asking them within the company for which I worked.

The Royal Navy came to the rescue! I spent two happy years working in a Naval hospital during which time my leadership was exercised, responsibilities increased and confidence encouraged. Here I found reward in the activity and very little in the salary. More importantly for my developing Christian faith, a group of young men and women joined together to establish an open Christian Fellowship. We began to challenge one another, to pray together, lead Bible studies, speak at public meetings and nurture our own Christian lives. Gestation was over: birth had taken place. It was not an easy birth in the rough and tumble of naval life. I was, again, vulnerable but this time there was a difference. This time I knew I was vulnerable because I was weak in a strong, tough environment and I had to learn the difficult lesson which confronts all young Christians. I had to learn to rely on God's faithfulness to me, but that was a lesson which was soon to come under great strain: unaware of it, I left the hospital with tuberculosis.

After leaving the Navy I had very much wanted to continue my medical studies but, I suppose because of my poor school record, my parents would not consider it a possibility. So it was back to commerce, but my despair was lifted when I met a Christian girl who was training to be a teacher. Pam and I eventually married but before then there was much to test both our love and our faith. I was a reasonably good rugby player and it was when I was training for the 1953 season that I collapsed. Diagnosis: tubercular pleurisy of the left lung. The last four months of that year were spent flat on my back fighting for my physical and my spiritual life; life which was only just beginning to make sense to me. What now? I was much too ill to think clearly and rationally. Surrounded by prayer and the careful attention of many doctors, the loving care of my mother and father, the deepening affection of my girlfriend, the support of many friends and the sensitive visits of the parish priest we came through the ordeal together.

Although at the time I did not realize it, there is no doubt in my mind now that those four months were a turning point in my life. As with any long journey there comes a time for re-fuelling; this was to be one of life's pit-stops. I had to learn, as it says in the Bible, that Christ's 'power is strongest when I am weak' but shall I ever be able to go so far as to say that 'I am most happy to be proud of my weaknesses'? I doubt it, but I will say that my illness led me to realize that 'when I am weak, then I am strong'. This suffering (and there were times when it was very painful suffering) was part of my Christian awakening; I was emerging into a real consciousness of my faith. Although I did not know it at the time, this was to serve me well in the years to come.

The hours were long during the early days as I lay sweating and dozing, too ill even to read, with just enough strength to take numerous tablets. I don't recall any fear. There was no bitterness but I did wonder, 'why?' As my health slowly improved so began a time of sharpened consciousness; I liked the solitude and I became acutely conscious (and sometimes impatient) of any sound that broke it. I still remember the joyful moment, when I was being taken from the house to an ambulance, when I again felt the wind on my face; the thrill of hearing the knock on the door, not knowing who was there; the pleasure of hearing birds singing by my window. God and I were close during these moments. I became more aware of, and sensitive to, my surroundings, discovering a perception which activity and familiarity had dulled.

After four months of almost complete physical inactivity 1954 saw slow, oh so very slow, improvements with the occasional setback (which was always difficult for my parents to accept). Where was God in all of this? Were there not other ways to give me time to pray, to read, to reflect? Perhaps there was no concealed reason; perhaps the actual suffering itself would be turned to good account. Did I though, really have to get so very, very close to death? Serious doubts began to batter my emerging faith; was this a test of its young strength? Did it matter anyway? Was it not the case that without some doubt my faith would not mature? Perhaps doubt is an essential ingredient in the spiritual life. I lay in my bed thinking that absolute certainty would be the death of my faith. Certainty would make my faith obsolete. Uncertainty would allow it to live.

I was changing, but what was changing me? My physical condition was obvious to everyone; I was gaining strength from the treatment. My spiritual frailty, evident to some, was responding to the challenge of my weakened state. I had always been an avid reader and now the time I had I used to read widely, to think critically and to analyze minutely. Imprisoned in my bed I was certainly inactive physically but there was a mental freedom. I developed an intellectual restlessness which was satisfied because there was time, and there were people who came to see me to talk, to reflect, to argue. My weakness was changing me because within it I was finding strength. I became more and more intellectually disturbed and although this period of illness, and the year which was still to come, were creative times in my life, they were to affect me deeply in the future. Yet, I still find it difficult not to associate two-and-a-half years in bed with wastefulness. Is that because I still have much to learn about living the Christian life to the full?

Was it a waste? Might it not, just conceivably, have been a God-given opportunity which I could have wasted? I do wonder whether the experience itself has influenced me in such a way that I can call it an opportunity, or perhaps even a privilege. After all, I know something which it is impossible for others who have not been through the experience to know. Suffering is a very private and personal experience which cannot be fully conveyed to anyone else. What is not experienced is not known. Isn't this why God came into the world, to demonstrate to us the extremes of love and suffering? Lying in bed I convinced myself of the privilege of suffering, and strength emerged from weakness.

My parish priest and I ranged widely in our discussions and we always prayed together during his visits. They were influential times and, with his guidance and the encouragement of Pam, I decided the time had arrived for my formal entry into the Anglican Church. So, one Sunday in November 1954, I was baptized at Morning Prayer in the parish church. Confirmation followed two weeks later and now I had two things both important to me in the development of my life as a Christian: a structure and a fellowship.

Pam and I were married in 1955 on the old St Thomas' Day in St Thomas' Church where her faith had been nurtured and developed rather earlier than mine. Often, as my faith faltered, she was there to support and encourage and we were to need all her resilience as after two years of marriage TB struck again. Another one-year pit-stop before I could move out of my tubercular twenties and into the thirties. Into what? I was gaining in physical and spiritual strength and two years of part-time study, often into the early morning hours, was providing me with a firmer intellectual base. With health restored, faith confirmed, knowledge expanded and love around me I was certainly gaining in strength but for what purpose? It was about this time that the parish priest who had been so often at my bedside asked me to speak in church about my faith and I recall using a variety of interpretations of the theme, 'A Certain Man'. Now the talking had to stop: the testing time had come.

I was seeking something more personally fulfilling than commerce so, even before receiving the results of the first national examination I'd ever taken, I left my job. Ten years before when Pam was studying at an Anglican college of education she introduced me to the principal who now took one of those risks which characterizes all fine leadership; she offered me a place to study education and theology. There were, not surprisingly, certain conditions which were soon to be met in the examination results. Pam and I had been married six years and I wondered whether we should put our marriage under the strain of separation. Pam had less doubt. We had learned that God does not provide easy solutions. College went well. For my theology dissertation I chose to write on the problem of human suffering; could I do otherwise?

With my twenties characterized by illness, behind me, my thirties were about to be distinguished by rapid change and stable faith. College student, orphan, teacher, father, Anglican Reader, Scout Commissioner, undergraduate, college lecturer, academic researcher. God seemed to have a full agenda for me. Could this be the same person who found school so tedious and so boring? What next? Pam and I talked about our future with close Christian friends, not to avoid the responsibility of decision making but to test whether or not I was dictating my own ambitions. Nearly all of my many roles involved some form of leadership. This was something I rarely, if ever, sought but it was a feature of my life which was to become more dominant during this period and beyond. After all the turmoil of my early life I would have been more than content to pursue a quiet academic life. Other people had other ideas. As we responded to them Pam and I liked to think that we were being obedient to

God's guidance which was made clear to us through others. What was certain was that he was using me in ways neither of us had ever remotely considered possible; somehow he had taken my weaknesses and given me a strength which I never sought, never anticipated and never, knowingly, rejected.

Work was not confined to this country. In 1963 I made the long and sometimes difficult journey to the remote Seychelles; there was no airport there in those days. On one of those beautiful Indian Ocean islands, Praslin, a young man, asked if he might take part in leading the worship which started each day of the Scout training course I was running. From that small start he went on to ordination, while another participant was on his way to becoming the Archbishop of the Indian Ocean. Although I did not know it at the time (there we go again!) this was to be the start of some extensive work overseas. Jamaica was soon followed by Lesotho and some sixteen other countries in Africa and the Middle East. I now had the chance to travel the world but, attractive though that was, I felt that I should not flit from one country to another but rather that I should exercise my Christian ministry with one people. I wanted to know them intimately, to learn their language, to understand their thinking, to experience their love, to share their faith.

So it was that the Basotho came to dominate my overseas work for twenty-one years as I exercised my profession through education, preached the word of the gospel through the Church and promoted the work of the gospel through development projects. Flying thousands of miles each year is no fun for me. I don't like travelling but I do like arriving, and to arrive among a people of another culture to share a common faith makes it all worthwhile. The Basotho have taught me much. I was soon to learn that if Christians are to be, as the Bible says, 'one body in Christ', it must involve sharing all that goes to make up our different lives. After many years the Basotho gave me one of their names, Ramosa, and with it a responsibility; it means 'father of mercy and kindness'.

Whilst all the overseas work was developing, my many roles at home continued to expand; college vice-principal, chairman of a public limited company, the chairmanship of committees galore and, since I believe that 'all work and no play makes Jack a dull boy', I qualified as a yachtmaster. God was making it quite clear that 'to whom much is given, of him much will be required; and of him to whom men commit much they will demand the more'. Demand there certainly was. Pam and I tried to meet it, relying more and more upon our faith. It wasn't easy. We wanted to give our two children, Edmund and Rachel, all the time they required in the difficult task of growing up. God had entrusted them to us and we knew that it was important to spend time with them although the nature of my overseas work meant that I was often away during the summer holidays. I always enjoyed our early family holidays and now I sometimes feel sad that I missed those when I was working overseas. Perhaps that is part of the cost of my Christian work but it has been a cost to both myself and my family.

When I was sailing my boat I soon learned that to navigate safely at sea it is essential to know both your starting position and your proposed destination. In my life, even when I had both those essential facts, I knew that I could never reach my destination solely by my own efforts. The longest of all my many journeys has taken me from an unknown starting point to a waypoint which I cannot distinguish, towards a destination which I cannot comprehend. On my sickbed I concluded that absolute certainty makes faith redundant. With so much stimulus from an uncertain future my faith, as it has already been, is and will be of crucial importance for the remainder of what has already been a long and very wonderful journey.

BISHOP JOSEPH IIDA

*F*ew people can tell at first-hand the story of
the dropping of the first atomic bomb. When I
heard Bishop Joseph tell his story I was profoundly
moved. Although he was from a Christian family,
Joseph's background was set in a culture that at best
treated Christians with suspicion and at worst labelled
them as spies and traitors. His home town of Sasebo
lies just thirty miles from Nagasaki.

Several years before the second atomic bomb was
dropped, the government had denounced Western
colonizing countries. It cannot have been easy for a
young Christian to level his country's mission with
what his heart told him was right. Part of Joseph's
story is of turmoil and dismay as much that was dear
to him was obliterated.

Yet Joseph's story is also a confident one as he
seeks to reconcile the events he witnessed with the idea
of a loving God – the God who led his people out of
the wilderness. The journeying people of the Old
Testament knew as much about despair as they did
about hope and Joseph clearly has an empathy with
them.

Joseph's story – and, indeed, his continuing journey – is important to me because it vividly demonstrates what can happen when people rely on God in difficult situations. It does not mean that the situation is completely understood, but neither is it passively accepted. Rather there is a determination to affirm a Christian identity in a fragile and distorted world.

The Pillar of Cloud and the Pillar of Fire

Quietness prevailed in the upstairs study room of the Naval Academy, located in Etajima Island about ten miles south of the city of Hiroshima. It was 6 August 1945, and a fine summer morning as usual. A bright cloudless blue sky almost seduced us to forget that it was wartime.

All of a sudden a purple flash of light dyed the air of the room, just like a large-scale short-circuit of electricity, or a direct thunderbolt. My classmates who were sitting by the windows told me later that they felt heat on their necks. a few seconds later a huge gust of wind struck the building and it shook as if there was an earthquake.

Naval officers are trained never to lose their nerve under any circumstances, and nobody moved nor made a noise. The few minutes' quietness was broken by a bugle order to 'Abandon Ship', so we rushed to the staircase to jump into the underground air-raid shelters. But lo and behold! We could see a mushroom cloud, furiously bubbling up against the blue sky.

But then nothing happened – there was no noise. So one by one, senior students first, we climbed up from the shelters and watched the cloud. At night it turned rosy grey, reflecting the fires in the city of Hiroshima caused by the bomb. The cloud stood there for about two days, and was gradually blown away by the eastward wind.

Without any association, the words 'pillar of cloud and pillar of fire' (from the book of Exodus in the Bible) popped up in my mind. I had once happily learned the story in Sunday school, but had later had hated the fact that I was born as the eldest son of a priest of the Anglican Church.

Christianity had been accused as the religion of the enemy countries before and during the war. The Anglican Church especially was persecuted, because of its association with England. Day and night, in schools and on streets, Christians were labelled as spies and traitors. Church buildings were stoned. My father was visited and persistently interrogated by members of the special security police, until I got into the Naval Academy, which might be reckoned by them as proof of patriotism in my family.

Nine days later the war was over and the Emperor declared an unconditional surrender. A week later, the Naval Academy was dissolved along with the disarmament of all military forces, and we had to go home. We went by cutter from the academy, landed at the southwest part of Hiroshima City and waited for a train. Finally a string of open coal cars came, and we got in. The train stopped at a station, the name of which I do not know even to this day, because there remained nothing to be identified but a platform.

Under the moonlight we saw the total devastation of the city. Nothing was left but piles of burned bricks and junk on the flat delta of the River Ota. There stood several burned trees like human hands crying for help against the black background of the Chugoku mountain range. Since it was more than a fortnight after the dropping of the bomb, we did not see even a single dead body on the ground, but the air was filled with the sickening stink of burned dead bodies. Some of us vomited.

I went back to my home town of Sasebo in Kyushu, thirty miles north of the city of Nagasaki – on which the second A-bomb was dropped three days after Hiroshima. I was sent by my father to Nagasaki to search for the family of the Anglican priest.

The whole day long, I searched for them in vain, until a man told me to climb up one of the surrounding hills and to search the other side of it. At the top of the hill I was astonished and caught my breath. The side of the slope of the hill that I had climbed from the harbour was total destruction; nothing was left but greyish piles of bricks. But the other side on which I now looked was full of greenery. Houses remained among the trees, untouched by the effects of the bomb which had taken the lives of another 200,000. Then some more words from the Bible struck me, 'I have set before you life and death, blessings and curses. Choose life so that you and your descendants may live' (The Old Testament book of Deuteronomy).

Four years before the A-bombs were dropped, the Japanese people had made a decision to make war against the Western colonizing countries and to become the leader of the Asian nations. Did not the whole nation rejoice when this was announced? We cannot blame only the then leaders of our nation. We all participated in that decision, although most of us had been deceived by the biased propaganda of the government.

We had made a wrong decision at that time. No kinds of conflict, international or domestic, had ever been solved by means of war and violence. We Japanese boasted that we were a superior race to all the other nations in Asia. But we had chosen the way of death. The scene before my eyes seemed to me the clear indication of the symbol of the two ways – the way of life, and the way of death. Later I found out that some of my classmates, including my best friend, had died at Nagasaki by the A-bomb.

After the war we were told that all the things we had been taught in school were false and full of errors. Most parts of the textbooks on Japanese history had to be blackened with ink, leaving only a few lines on each page. We had been taught that the Emperor was a living god, and we had to worship him every morning, but he declared that he was not a god, only a human being. Militarism, totalitarianism, colonialism, nationalism, racism, on which my previous education was wholly based, were condemned by the loud voices of the so-called democratic intelligentsia, who had been silenced during the war.

I felt as though the ground on which I had been standing crumbled down into an unfathomable abyss. For a sixteen-year-old boy this was hard to swallow. What had I been doing in all those days? Was it for nothing? Had we been deceived all through those sixteen years? Who was I? What should I do? What was my purpose for life? What was the human being after all, who could have done such horrible things – the Nanking holocaust by the Japanese army, the genocide attempt by Nazi Germany? Was there any purpose in this universe? I began a long pilgrimage in search of identity and the purpose of life. All the school years, then senior high, university, theological seminary, were motivated by this existential quest.

In the condition of half-starvation after the war, my spiritual struggle continued. A vague idea of what I should do with my life was emerging slowly in my mind. I felt as though I should be doing something to serve the people in this turmoil and meaninglessness. And at one time I was so attracted by the ideals of Marxist theory that I almost made up my mind to join the Communist Party. At the YMCA's summer seminar, the theme of which was 'Christianity versus Marxism', I found myself defending the Christian church from the assaults of my poorly informed Marxist friends, instead of advocating Marxism which was my original intention for attending the seminar. Inside my mind was a sheer mess. I had to get rid of Christianity!

After the seminar, I spent the rest of the summer vacation reading the Bible from the first page of the Book of Genesis to the last page of the Book of Revelation, so that I could criticize Christianity. Compared with the theoretical nature of the Marxist documents, the Bible was not written in logical form and even contained many obvious contradictions. But I was caught by it; not by its logic, but by something else. You may call it the Spirit.

Both of them, Christianity and Marxism alike, aim at an ideal state of being – called 'the kingdom of God' in the Bible. But I found out at that time the fundamental difference between the two – the motivations from which all their actions flowed. While Marxists' actions were motivated by love toward the oppressed labourer and hatred towards bourgeois, Christians were motivated by the unconditional love of God, even toward their enemies. In the Gospel of John, it says, 'God so loved the world that he gave his only Son, so that everyone who believes in him may not perish but have eternal life.'

Suppose you were able to build an ideal state of being on this earth in which the labourers who had been oppressed now possessed the power. Who can tell that their achievements, motivated by hatred, would not then be overthrown by the hatred of those who were now the oppressed? Someone's hatred will surely create hatred in the hearts of those who are hated.

From then on, Jesus became my Saviour and my Lord. But I believed that he should not only be my Saviour, but also the Saviour of all the human beings in all the nations which had fought one another in the past war. I had been given a mission to tell this story of God's profound love.

One other thing I struggled with was why the words 'pillar of cloud and pillar of fire' had struck me when I first saw the mushroom cloud over Hiroshima. They came from the Book of Exodus, and there the cloud was the symbol of God's protection and liberation of the Hebrew people from slavery in Egypt. Perhaps it symbolized freedom for the people of South East Asian countries who had been occupied and oppressed by the Japanese, and for the American soldiers who were so afraid of the coming combat for the main islands of Japan. But how could the pillar of cloud and the pillar of fire, caused by the A-bomb which killed so many people and caused so much destruction, be a symbol of salvation for us?

I have struggled for a long time with this question. But now I have a tentative answer. Although I am not suggesting by any means that those who were killed were particularly guilty, the A-bomb was God's judgment for the whole Japanese nation on its racial prejudice and arrogance, which had resulted in the casualty of more than two million people and devastation of South East Asian countries and Korea, on the one hand. But on the other hand, it was God's act of mercy on our nation, because we were delivered from racism, nationalism, totalitarianism and militarism. It was God's grace. His grace came with his judgment at the same time. To repent, we had to sacrifice the precious lives of half a million innocent people.

I am not justifying the use of any indiscriminately destructive weapons. Even existing nuclear weapons can exterminate the whole human race several times. As the only nation in the world which has actually suffered from them, we have an almost destined duty not to forget the experience and to oppose the production, use, and keeping of such weapons. But one cannot live on forever cherishing resentment. The past is past and no one can change it. The past was stamp-approved by the Lord of history. In so saying I am not passing any moral judgments but an ontological one. If we are not forgiving to those who dropped the A-bombs, how can we be forgiven our acts of the sneak attack on Pearl Harbour and of malicious treatment of the people of Korea, and East and South East Asia?

I believe that we are required to 'forget what lies behind, strain forward to what lies ahead'. Having learned from these experiences, our nation firmly decided that we would never again declare war against any nation as the means of solving international conflict. Our national constitution declares this point very clearly. Although we have some military, its sole purpose is self-defence. We do not allow them to go abroad to engage in fighting. One of the reasons for the miraculous economic success of our nation out of the ashes of wartime is, I believe, the fact that we have never invested more than one per cent of Gross National Product to the expenditures of armament, so that we have been able to invest heavily in education and the welfare of the people.

The lesson I learned from Hiroshima was this. Almighty God, who created the whole universe and sustains all things within it, is the God who observes the misery of his people, hears their cry on account of oppression, knows their suffering, and comes down to free them. All through history, when necessary, he did send, does send, and will send his agents to fulfil his purpose so that his justice prevails on this earth. He sent Abraham, Moses, prophets and at the end of time will send Jesus Christ. But he was also able to use King Cyrus and stones on the wayside to do his will. God is working in this world. He is the Lord of history. He is always challenging us through worldly events.

We Japanese Christians, though a tiny minority, have a great task to do. We must work against the grievous resurgence of the ghost of Emperor worship which once led the whole nation into the abyss of narrow-minded nationalism and racism at the cost of other nations. Having achieved economic success, has the Japanese nation as a whole, forgotten the bitter lesson of 'the pillar of cloud and the pillar of fire'?

My constant prayer is words from the Lord's Prayer, prayed by Jesus: 'Your will be done on earth as in heaven. Forgive us our sins as we forgive those who sin against us.'

SIMON MAYO

*O*ne of my greatest concerns is to find ways in
which the church can be involved with young
people, many of whom have little contact with the
Christian faith. The traditional verbal presentation of
Christianity may have little relevance to young people
who are more at home with visual or musical images.

Simon has for many years been highly successful
as a Radio 1 presenter and his forays into TV and
writing have brought him further success in an
industry which drops its 'favoured few' as quickly as
they emerge into stardom. Simon has had to wrestle
with being a 'successful' Christian, and the tensions
which that brings.

I have valued Simon's refreshing approach and his
insights into a generation from which, for the most
part, I am remote. The honesty of his reflections has
caused me to think afresh about the impact and
relevance of the Christian message. Perhaps, most of
all, Simon reminds me that although some young
people do not go to church, this does not mean that
they are unspiritual. Christians should meet people on
their own terms, and not expect them to be familiar
with the church. This is important if young people are
to encounter the reality and wonder of God's kingdom.

Contemporaries
of Christ

Thrills, as the reader is, I hope, aware, come in many shapes and sizes. In no particular order, my thrills have been winning the FA Cup in 1991 (not personally, although I like to kid myself), getting married, appearing on 'The Generation Game', joining Radio 1, being present at my two kids' births and being asked to do a fifteen-minute talk on Radio 4. This was a thrill because my parents only ever really listen to Radio 4 and so for the first time they could listen to their elder son without having to turn the radio down when it got to the noisy or embarrassing bits. I was asked to reflect on the passion story – Jesus' suffering and death – from the lofty, if somewhat grubby, perch of a Radio 1 DJ. I had been selected apparently because I was a contemporary of Christ.

Now, if it is ever suggested that you might like to consider yourself 'a contemporary of Christ', your immediate thought would not, I believe, be a particularly theological one. My day started at 4.00a.m., and I took the suggestion to mean that after five years of presenting the breakfast show, I was at last beginning to look 2,000 years old as well as feel it.

No. Apparently the theory is, that at 34, I was within a few months of the age that Christ was when he was crucified, and therefore we were contemporaries. This, I don't mind telling you, had never occurred to me before. I felt annoyed at all the anniversaries I'd missed. I could have had a baptismal party when I was thirty, a party for 5,000 when I was thirty-one and a donkey derby at thirty-two. Come to think of it, I could have had a party in the temple – without my parents – when I was twelve, and had a quick trip to Egypt when just a few months old. My life seemed quite dull in comparison.

I read recently in one of those embarrassingly readable women's magazines, that a man in his thirties is considered to be at the peak of his powers – physically, intellectually and sexually. This – if true – is a great disappointment to me and my wife. My peak – just like the 'John Major-a-gram' in an episode of television's 'Drop The Dead Donkey' – clearly arrived, hung around for a bit, and then left, without anyone noticing.

Your fourth decade of life certainly does seem to carry a burden of responsibility. Apart from anything else, you're suddenly aware, perhaps for the first time, of your passing years. Mick Jagger (of the Rolling Stones) said recently, 'There are certain times which come with men. When you're thirty-one, thirty-two you get this Christ-syndrome. When I was that age I thought "I'm neglecting my education". So I started to read again. And I went through this thing of trying to understand quite heavy things. Difficult to understand books. Back to philosophy and religion and novels that didn't come off the racks at airports.'

Even if you're not a multi-millionaire rock star, frightening thoughts do start arriving in your head, just when it's terribly inconvenient. If you're not married yet, it's getting late. If you're planning to have children, you'd better get on with it. If you're going to buy some property, why didn't you start years ago! If you're going to have a decent career, you should be at least halfway up your chosen ladder by now. So, a 33-year-old ex-carpenter and itinerant preacher, with no kids, no wife, no house and no prospects, who gets arrested and then killed has – even in these dismal Nineties – to be judged a failure.

Even *Hello* magazine, with its famed ability to 'talk up' the lives and careers of even the most tawdry celebrities, would have been hard pressed to write a glowing paragraph, never mind a whole article. Jesus of Nazareth may have been the founder of the biggest and most influential religion of all time, but to any impartial observer of events in the Palestine of around AD30, this man was a failure. A few interesting friends and a way with words perhaps, but still a failure.

Ted Turner, the owner of the staggeringly successful Cable News Network in the US, is reported to have said that Christianity is a religion for failures. The events of Holy Week that culminated with Christ's crucifixion on Good Friday can certainly be read that way. Betrayed by one of his own circle of friends to the soldiers of an occupying power, the desertion of his other disciples, the denial – three times – by Simon Peter that he ever knew him, the corrupt and illegal show trials and the long and tortuous criminal death. Perhaps Ted was right.

But then perhaps Ted is the kind of person who chooses not to read the last chapter of a P.D. James mystery or switches off before the final splendid *dénouement* of an 'Inspector Morse' story. So as far as the disciples were concerned, it was a disastrous failure. For Jesus' other followers – those who admired him from a discreet and respectable distance of course – it was a catastrophe. For the citizens of Jerusalem who had got so excited when he arrived just seven days before, and who expected a miraculous liberator, it was a calamity. But as it turned out, it wasn't much of a victory for the authorities either.

It was only Jesus who seemed to know exactly what was going to happen and why. He had told his disciples three times that he had to go to Jerusalem, where he would be betrayed, and then crucified. In case they still hadn't got it, he went on: 'I tell you the truth, unless a kernel of wheat falls to the ground and dies, it remains only a single seed. But if it dies, it produces many seeds... Now my heart is troubled and what shall I say? Father, save me from this hour? No, it was for this very reason I came to this hour.'

So while the events of that week must have seemed a complete fiasco – a whirlwind of chaos – Jesus alone appears to keep his single-mindedness and clarity of vision. His crucifixion, agonizing, gut-wrenching and God-less as it was, I believe to be his ultimate success.

On a slightly less heavenly level, there is another success to enjoy here. As I'm a radio fanatic, my heroes have always been the great communicators. In amongst the Gilbert and Sullivan records and assorted Beethoven symphonies, my parents would regularly play another favourite, 'The Voice of Richard Dimbleby'. I had never heard the original broadcasts of course, but the power of his words and his immaculate delivery have stayed with me ever since. Other heroes have followed: the peerless Alistair Cooke, Radio 2's ultimate 'friend behind the microphone' John Dunn, Birmingham DJ Les Ross – one of the sharpest broadcasters I've ever heard. The late Peter Jones, Radio 2's great sports commentator, James Naughtie, Noel Edmonds, David Frost, Alan Freeman – I could fill this chapter with nothing but names! All of them inspired me to get involved in this broadcasting business in the first place and all of them have, or had, the gift of finding the right phrase at the right time. The effect on the listener can be devastating.

There is a fine line, of course, between what is perceived as success and what is perceived as failure. In the radio and television world that I try to inhabit, success is topping opinion polls, making creative and original programmes, collecting awards, amassing a large audience and at the same time achieving critical acclaim. I am, like most broadcasters I know, deeply insecure about most of my work. If audience figures are down, if I get a poor review or I fail to win an award I was nominated for, I get grumpy, depressed and bad-tempered. If, though, the figures are good, the reviews are at least bearable or I win some worthless piece of plastic to put on my bookcase, the world is a wonderful place again. For a broadcaster, though, a certain degree of popular acceptance and approval is essential. There is no point after all, in broadcasting to yourself. Although there were times in my hospital and university radio days, when I'm sure that's exactly what I was doing.

But since those heady days of transmitting to the slumbering occupants of Southlands Hospital in Shoreham and the just as slumbering students at Warwick University, I have to be honest and admit that I have sought, and continue to seek, both success and popularity. It sounds crass to just come out and put it like that, but it is indisputably true. The problem is that they don't always go together. While popularity is largely to do with numbers, success is not. Van Gogh was not a popular painter in his lifetime but his creations were, artistically, hugely successful. Most people have records in their collection that no one else has heard of, but are, so the owners would argue, little masterpieces. I happen to think that my hospital radio shows were successful – they achieved the aim of providing appropriate entertainment for hospitalized old folk. 'Popular' though is not a label that was ever attached to them, largely because most of my audience would hear one of the shows and then die before the next one was broadcast.

My point is that I'm trying to drive a somewhat reluctant wedge between two words that always seem to be lumped together. Success does not equal popularity. Jesus ultimately succeeded and yet he didn't seek, nor did he attain, great levels of popularity. Indeed the story of Jesus' temptation suggests to me there might be something almost demonic about great acclaim. Jesus has been in the desert for forty days, without food, and is being tempted by the devil. At the top of a very high mountain, Jesus is shown all the kingdoms of the world in their glory. 'All these,' says the devil, 'I will give you, if you will only fall down and pay me homage.' But Jesus says 'Out of my sight, Satan! Scripture says "You shall do homage to the Lord your God and worship him alone".'

I see Jesus being offered here wealth, comfort, and all the popularity he could ever ask for. I'm sure Jesus was tempted – being human, how could he not be – but what the world would have acclaimed as great success and fortune, to him would have been defeat and disaster. The film *Jesus of Montreal*, which follows the story of an actor chosen to play the part of Christ in an Easter passion play, uses incidents in the actor's life, in splendid allegories of incidents in Christ's life. In the film, the up-and-coming actor is shown the whole of Montreal from the top of a skyscraper by his lawyer – an interesting parallel. The lawyer tells him that if he makes it and stays with him, the whole of Montreal will be eating out of his hand and everything he could ever have wished for will be his.

Now without suggesting that the entire legal profession is in league with Satan or that if you are the recipient of universal praise and acclamation, you're demonically possessed – Cliff Richard would be worried – there is a somewhat disconcerting point here. Although the concept of 'celebrity' is exceedingly biblical, it is always connected with biblical-scale problems. The superstars of the Bible – Saint Paul, King David, Abraham, John the Baptist, Adam and Eve – had problems that would make our most outrageous hellraisers quite envious: debauchery, jail, adultery, murder, attempted murder, alcohol abuse, wild lifestyle – it's all there!

There seems to be something about power, wealth, luxury and the attendant status it all brings, that has the ability to render the holder less human, less open, less touchable, less responsive. Demonic or not, if you're put on a pedestal and adored, the outcome can demean both the worshipper and the worshipped. Apart from anything else, the view from the pedestal is quite attractive. The thought of having to climb down from it is increasingly unpleasant. No matter what compromises you've made getting up there, there's a whole new set just waiting to be tried if you want to stay.

So, if widespread popularity can mean sell-out, it's no wonder that Jesus found himself at the top of a death list. The religious authorities hated and feared him, the Roman authorities acquiesced in his execution, many in his home town wanted nothing to do with him. The Gospel of Matthew records a whole town turning up to plead with Jesus to move on and leave the region altogether because they were scared of his 'magic powers'. Even his own brothers were embarrassed by him.

It is true, of course, that large crowds followed him everywhere he went, often to the point of distraction. He was a celebrity – he was the talk of the town. And the temple. And the palace. When Jesus stood trial before Herod, it's quite clear that the Tetrarch was thrilled to be meeting such a superstar. Luke reports that he was 'greatly pleased' to be meeting Jesus and had wanted to meet him for 'some time'. Jesus' reputation as a wonder worker had clearly spread far and wide and Herod had been hoping to experience a miracle or two. As he sings in the musical *Jesus Christ Superstar*: 'Prove to me that you're no fool – walk across my swimming pool!' But when Jesus doesn't oblige, and even refuses to speak, Herod turns against him, resorting to mockery and cheap abuse. This isn't popularity, it's a short-lived curiosity.

There's an impression of superficiality about some of the apparent popularity that Jesus had. When he rode into Jerusalem on a donkey, the Gospel of Matthew records a very large crowd welcoming Jesus, running around, shouting, spreading their coats on the road, and generally behaving in a splendidly juvenile manner. 'When Jesus entered Jerusalem,' Matthew says, 'the whole city was stirred and asked "Who is this?" '

But it doesn't take very long for this enthusiasm to evaporate. When Pilate, halfway through his quizzing of Jesus, turns to the crowd to offer them either his release or a notorious criminal called Barabbas, the call is for Barabbas. American President Bill Clinton was nonplussed when his support waned dramatically in eight weeks. Jesus' had gone in five days.

His final success may have been imminent, but his popularity had withered away. In those last desperate hours of torture and death, the world might have been turning upside down, but with the exception of a few women supporting Jesus' mother, he was on his own.

2,000 years on, and there's a familiar feel to the popular acceptance of Jesus. Never before has it been quite so common to hear his name used in everyday conversation. Jesus Jones, The Jesus and Mary Chain and Jesus Loves You are all rock bands. In 1992 Genesis had a hit song called 'Jesus He Knows Me'. None of this indicates any acceptance or approval of Jesus Christ, merely an acknowledgment of the value of using a trendy name. Jean Paul Gaultier, Georgio Armani, Che Guevara, Jesus Christ.

Religion, religious imagery, artefacts and language are high fashion. Madonna has always made a big issue out of wearing a crucifix – she says having a naked man around your neck is sexy. Depeche Mode produced an album entitled *Songs of Faith and Our Own Redemption*. One of the world's most popular artists is the artist formerly known as Prince, a man clearly obsessed with both sex and religion. He is as at home writing about the cross and its importance in his life as he is writing about oral sex. At the Aids benefit concert for Freddie Mercury at Wembley, David Bowie – in what must have been the rock world's most unusual and unlikely show-stopper – got down on one knee and recited the Lord's Prayer – thees, thous, trespasses and all. Here was a man, who amongst many other things is known for introducing the pink jockstrap to Japan, happily leading the most public pray-in since Jimmy Swaggart. Now it might be that he was making a completely sincere statement, and not having a vast catalogue of religious songs to fall back on, responded in the only way he could think of. Equally it might have been a cynical and stage-managed publicity stunt. But either way, it is yet another indication of Jesus' pseudo-popularity.

In the same way that Jesus exposed the superficial level of interest of a rich young ruler, so too he would see through the sham of his current popularity. Not that he'd waste much time over it – his passions and commitments would have him busy elsewhere. One of Canada's greatest singers, Bruce Cockburn, wrote a song once called 'Cry of a Tiny Babe'. In it he tells the Christmas story and includes the line: 'It wasn't to the palace that the Christ-child comes, but to hobos, street people, hookers and bums'.

Failures, in other words. People to whom success is a bus shelter to spend the night, a can of cider for company and perhaps a few quid for a night's work. 'Christianity is a religion for failures,' says Ted Turner. In a way that he didn't realize – perhaps he was right.

ALISON MOORE

*I*n this collection of stories I wanted to introduce
readers both to people who are well known, and to
others who are representatives of 'ordinary' Christians.
Alison is such a representative. In my days as vicar of
St Nicholas' church in Durham, Alison was a very
significant leader. She has both a deep spirituality, and
refreshing common sense. Her intellect, clarity in
thinking and sheer enthusiasm became increasingly
evident as she became more involved in the church.
She also provided a most valuable balance to the more
radical proposals of the vicar when he was inclined to
let an idea race too far ahead of the feasible!

Alison is a gifted person with a very full life –
teacher, wife, mother, counsellor – yet that has not
impeded her ability to listen and to radiate a warmth
that needs no words. But what especially impressed
me about Alison was her spiritual perception, and her
sensitivity which could in a moment transform any
difficult meeting. Her story reveals how God can use
people when they are open to him. It is a story of
identity, and of finding how faith can be personal as
well as 'inherited' from the older generation. It shows,
also, how the intellect cannot be the sole means of

discovery and Christian faith.

Many will recognize parts of Alison's faith journey, and will be able to agree with her discoveries and convictions. They will also recognize the feelings and conflicts around her journey.

'Yes, Lord'

How would you describe me? I am in my forties, a housewife, a marriage counsellor, a quilter, an intellectual, a musician, a mother to four boys, Geoff's wife, a teacher, a gardener... I recently came across a nursery school report from when I was three, which commented on my 'strong religious sense', and all four decades of my life have been lived with an awareness of God. My life has been a journey of faith, rather than a step from unbelief to faith.

In the Sixties I went to a Billy Graham rally. Although some people feel there is too much emotion at these events, it was just right for me. The Anglican church I belonged to was aesthetic but unemotional, and at the rally the part of me that longed for adventure and challenge was stirred. Billy Graham made clear how 'new life' as a Christian meant forgiveness and the chance to start again every day – so there is hope.

Before I went to university, I spent six months in France as an au pair. I arrived in Paris full of confidence, which was somewhat shaken when I found myself working for a wealthy family who had no interest in me beyond making sure I looked after their children properly. There was a long postal strike in England, so my reams of homesick letters were finally delivered in one great parcel to my poor parents when someone was visiting London. In my distress I realized how much my faith had depended on being with like-minded Christian friends. My prayers, like my French vocabulary, became extremely down to earth!

So I was ready for student life in Oxford. I became heavily involved with the Christian Union, and at the same time developed a busy social life, particularly because women were in the distinct minority at college. I used to fall in love with someone different each year, and it was always unrequited! Those years in Oxford passed in a glorious jumble of English literature, Christian Union, friends, parties, walks and music. I knew little of the life outside, neither Oxford, nor Britain, nor the world. Each summer I helped at a Christian holiday party for girls, where my understanding of God grew as I had to explain my faith to younger people. I would go home in the vacations, happily exhausted, and recover through sleeping and days of solitary dressmaking. I was pretty self-satisfied, and must have been insufferable for the family to live with. My sister and brother were teenagers at the time, yet I remember almost nothing about them, so wrapped up was I in my own life.

I sometimes wonder, looking back, if I am a little hard on the person I was then. After all, there is nothing wrong with enjoying life and savouring the good things. Perhaps I could not have been different until I had grown up a bit more. Yet I can't help feeling that the Christian environment I was in played a part: its concentration on the personal aspects of spirituality meant that I was unaware that there were other ways than evangelism for expressing faith, other demands Christ makes of those who are part of a privileged society. All these issues had to wait several years before I was ready to address them. Immediately after Oxford, I set off to Durham to train as a teacher.

From a top-floor room in Oxford, overlooking the river in one direction and beautiful gardens in the other, I moved to an ex-mining village outside Durham City. Here my window had a good view of the goats tethered on common land and the men-only bar at the Working Men's Club opposite! I became a Methodist for the year, and was warmly welcomed by the small congregation. 'Will you come for your dinner?' said one lady, and from there began a life-long friendship, as she and her husband took me in, almost as an extra daughter. Mr Sharp had been a local preacher in the Methodist church for years – over fifty years before he died in his seventies. He meticulously prepared a new sermon every quarter, and delivered it grippingly in each of the churches he visited. Mrs Sharp baked wonderful cakes and pies for tea, and always had enough to give away. She looked after anyone who needed a hand. Mr Sharp took great delight in initiating me into north-eastern dialect and customs. Their faith was self-giving, generous and humorous, though at the same time they didn't suffer fools gladly.

I was glad of their friendship in that training year, for I had mixed feelings about teaching. The theoretical side was fine – I soaked it up. Translating it into practice was quite another matter. I had had the same problem when I had tried skiing: I could never master the art of turning corners, although in my imagination I did it perfectly.

So teaching practice involved some basic learning for me too. 'Don't flick paint,' I said gently to a junior class; the next moment paint was flying everywhere! At the senior school I made the fatal mistake of laughing at the class clown instead of sending him out. Yet, at the same time, I did feel at home in front of a group, and I enjoyed explaining things and drawing the children out. So I always had a love-hate relationship with the job.

On good days I was on top of the world. I loved the challenge of engaging the attention of a new class every forty minutes. I worked out unorthodox solutions with an unruly older class: the disruptive children sat at the back playing cards so that I could get on with teaching the willing ones; if the rebels abused the agreement they were sent to the deputy head. And the children responded to the fact that I never victimized them or bore grudges. During these years, too, there was plenty to challenge my faith outside the classroom, for this was when George Carey was our vicar at St Nicholas' Church in Durham, and we embarked on a major building project, which I threw myself into with enthusiasm.

I taught for five years, and for some time after that I was unable to speak about the experience without distancing myself through jokes. When I was at last able to think about why that might be, I came to various conclusions. Firstly, my inability to 'succeed' in orthodox terms at teaching was probably not entirely my own fault; working in other schools might have been different, and I was probably better at relating to the children than I gave myself credit for. But more importantly, my Christian faith had not equipped me adequately for the experience of failure. I think my understanding was that to be a good Christian, I must be good at my job: success as Christian = success at job. In the Bible there are exhortations to strive to do your best, but there is also much about failure and weakness. I needed to understand more about that.

In the meantime, while teaching, I had met and married Geoff, and two years later Jonathan arrived. This was a new world indeed! They say that children are great levellers. As I walked round Durham doing my shopping after Jonathan was born, aching with exhaustion, I understood this for the first time. I would eye people in a new light, assessing whether they had been up for half the night too. I remember a weekend away with a large group of people from church. The children woke so early that Geoff had to take them out so that they didn't wake others. By six o'clock they were playing on the nearest beach! The following morning it was my turn, so we went downstairs to a meeting room with some toys. When an older parent went past us into breakfast with a cheerful comment about 'those early mornings', I had been up for three hours. I could barely manage a polite smile, I felt so sick with tiredness and very isolated. The constant exhaustion felt like an endless dark tunnel.

In those years of small children I found that most good advice on how to keep my spiritual life going became irrelevant. 'Get up half an hour earlier... Find a place where you can be on your own...' As for the hymn that tells us to 'let our ordered lives confess the beauty of your peace...', that was obviously not written by someone who had the full-time care of small children!

What should I do? When my entire middle-class culture, my education and also my Christian background promoted the virtues of control, order, discipline and achievement, how could I adapt to a life of disorder, chaos and no lasting achievement? I envied Geoff when he spent time on a DIY job: the results were permanent – the shelf was up. Whereas I spent my time ironing or cooking or nappy changing, and felt as though I was building sand-castles on the beach: the results were swept away daily by the tide. At its worst, I felt like the sorcerer's apprentice in the Disney cartoon, almost drowned by the floods and powerless to shift them.

Early on I changed the way I approached my spiritual life. The Bible does talk about discipline and order, but Christ himself seems to be very flexible, concentrating more on generosity of spirit, and self-denying love. He often used ordinary domestic examples to show God's ways of working. He was born into an ordinary family – so it seemed to me that Christ must identify with the messiness of family life. As he grew up, he must have known about nappy changing and meal preparation and family disagreements.

Gradually, I stopped seeing my busy life as a block cutting me off from God, and started viewing it more as a sort of living parable. Because the job of looking after small children demands unselfishness, it is, by its very nature, a way of sharing in the life of Christ. This was true, even if I could manage no formal devotional acts, and in this realization I felt held and warmed by God's love.

There were other lifelines too in those years. One was a weekly women's group where we helped maintain each other's sanity by talking about our experiences with our children and thrashing out all sorts of issues from potty training to feminism, education to the church, prayer to politics. Another lifeline was a slim volume by Angela Ashwin, *Heaven In Ordinary*. She was both a Christian and a mother. The book had tiny chapters that even the most exhausted parent could read before falling asleep. And she had lots of sensible and profound ideas for making the most of meeting God in the ordinary things of life.

From that book came the idea of the one- or two-word prayer that can be uttered at any time. Mine became 'Yes, Lord!' I would say it happily while enjoying the glorious moments of motherhood: sharing a joke with a three year old; reading a book in a comfortable chair while the baby breast-fed contentedly; shopping at the supermarket with the toddler in the trolley and the baby in a papoose, gazing at all the bright lights and colours; watching a bath full of happy children. Then I would say it reluctantly, through clenched teeth, in those other moments, when the chaos and bad temper were overwhelming. 'Yes, Lord,' when one child had a dirty nappy, one was throwing a tantrum and the other needed to be at school in five minutes; when my only target for the day was to do some ironing and even that got squeezed out; when my irritability spilled over at every turn and everything the children did was wrong; when I envied other people's freedom. 'Yes, Lord' was the only statement of faith I could muster. It was a shorthand way of saying, 'I do believe you have called me to this; this is the stuff of ordinary life; you had an ordinary life too.'

During this decade of small children, two subjects

came up in our women's group. The first was to do with us as consumers. We were comfortable, middle-class Christians; what were we to make of the big questions in the Bible about justice, freedom from oppression and feeding the hungry? One morning we were talking, drinking coffee and feeding babies while debating our views. Jill's husband Graham, who worked at home, joined us for a while. When I said, 'But I can't do anything. I'm only an ordinary housewife,' he challenged me. 'Every time you buy a jar of coffee,' he said, 'you are making a choice. You choose whether to buy a brand from a big multi-national where the producers are unjustly treated, or coffee that is fairly traded.'

That conversation was a revelation. Much as I hated the term, there was no escaping the fact that I *was* a consumer. Being a Christian consumer meant more than being generous with my possessions to my immediate neighbours and friends. There was also a responsibility to the more distant 'neighbour' who had been involved in producing those possessions. This shift from being a passive consumer to attempting to be an active one, was very important.

The other subject we tackled was a thorny one – feminism. We were not at all sure what a proper Christian outlook on the subject was, and invited a friend to come and lead the discussion. I remember saying tentatively, 'Well, I'm not a feminist, but...,', and she cut in with 'But in fact you are!' I meant that I did not see myself as aggressive or man-hating. She was rightly giving the word its proper meaning: I was, after all, female, and glad to be so; I took for granted the equality of the sexes; I was aware of some of the injustices that women suffer in our paternalistic culture. So I stopped apologizing for any 'feminist' opinions, and began to state them more firmly. Jesus said nothing to support male dominance and female obedience; rather, the picture is of a radical respect for everyone, regardless of gender.

Thoughts about the place of women in society set me wondering what the links were between my view of myself as a woman and my view of how to live out my faith. In the early Eighties I had started to train as a marriage counsellor with Relate. After one of the residential training weekends a tutor described me as 'manipulative'. I was furious and felt wounded and misunderstood; I wept in front of my personal supervisor who had the job of passing on the report. Looking back, I did have reason to be angry, but at the same time, the wretched man did me a service: he had put his finger on something important about the way I related to people. I had achieved much of my success in getting on with others by being pleasant; I was likeable, charming, made people feel good about themselves. In other words, I did manipulate them so that they couldn't fail to like me. This, I now know, is common among women and goes with feeling uncomfortable about rejection, conflict and confrontation. For years, although I could take leadership roles perfectly happily, I was almost incapable of returning faulty goods to a shop. It is not difficult to see what attracted me to my husband Geoff: he had the double qualities of seeing through my charm and being able to ask people politely to stop smoking in the non-smoking compartments of trains!

The revelations about 'manipulation' needed a lot of thought. Hadn't my Christian background taught me that it was right and proper to be pleasant, likeable, and helpful? Wasn't it thoroughly 'Christian' to make people feel good about themselves, pouring oil on troubled waters? If these were characteristics common to many women, and questionable ones at that, perhaps my whole Christian life had been a sham. Perhaps I had been deaf to the tougher demands of faith, only hearing what I wanted to hear. Maybe also there had been a lack in my Christian education, with too much emphasis on gentle love and not enough on hard justice. Whatever the reason, that tutor gave God a means of challenging me and enlarging my view of myself.

But not all the ways in which I expressed my faith were misguided. My attempts to be pleasant stemmed from a real interest in people and a desire to show love. I felt a particular affinity with children who were not immediately attractive, because as a young child I was always larger and lumpier than my contemporaries, growing like Alice in Wonderland to my adult size by the time I was ten. I remember the wistful envy I felt towards the other neat little girls, as adults were drawn warmly towards them. They seemed to forget that I was a little girl too, inside, and so I soon compensated by acting responsibly and older than my age. I think I vowed then that I would always follow my parents' example and take notice of the less attractive person, knowing that for him or her the hug or joke or compliment is that much more important.

Although the energetic activity of my life suited me in many ways, one year I decided that the noise and busy-ness was getting beyond a joke. My head, as well as my life, tended to be full of so many things that it was difficult to distinguish the important from the ephemeral. So, over several weeks, I took myself off to our spare room, and spent time attempting to be quiet. Eventually an inner silence of a sort established itself.

One important thing to emerge from those weeks of silent sessions was a deep and solid affirmation of my creative side. I had always enjoyed doing things with my hands: drawing, knitting, sewing, as well as looking at pictures and listening to music. These occupied the edges of my life: it always felt self-indulgent to be enjoying them, so they only took place when everything else had been seen to. But then I was struck that it is the story of creation that comes first in the Bible. And gradually I've had a change of attitude, and the creative has moved into the mainstream of my life. A weekly patchwork and quilting class inspires me; the sewing machine now lives out permanently on a table; browsing through pictures or textiles can happen on a weekday as well as on holiday.

And then we had a complete surprise. That spring we found that I was expecting another child! I had been planning my future, expecting to give much more time to marriage counselling once the three boys were at school, and here was God reminding me – rather dramatically – that the future always belongs to him. I was planning more activity; he made it impossible. So during that pregnancy and in the months that followed Daniel's birth, I savoured the experience, and deeply enjoyed just 'being' with the last baby.

This enforced change of plan gave me the opportunity to question everything. I had reached that infamous midpoint in life, between 35 and 40, when you can see the end point of life as well as the beginning. What was the future to hold? I'd spent twenty years happily being busy and organizing things: was I to spend the next twenty years the same way? Was that a necessary way to obey God?

The idea of 'being' yourself in response to God as much as 'doing' things, was at last beginning to make sense to me. It couldn't have come earlier. So in the five years after our fourth child's birth, I retired from all church committees, took a long-term sabbatical from Relate and, as a foil to domesticity, I started a theology course as well as the patchwork and quilting. Then I waited. Instead of making my own plans, I waited to see what would come from God for my future.

Now, all four of our sons are at school. I have returned to marriage counselling and continued theology. Quilting projects continue to bubble up both in my head and on the sewing machine. However, most of my time is still spent in the ordinary hubbub of family life.

To all of this, and to the future, I still say, 'Yes Lord.'

BRIAN PEARSON

*B*rian joined my staff at a time when I was looking
for ways to be more involved in reaching into
local communities while fulfilling the more traditional
administrative role of a diocesan bishop. I needed a
colleague who would support me in adapting a
somewhat radical approach to my ministry. Later, I
learned that this was what had prompted Brian to
apply for the job.

Brian has become a great friend who has many
gifts. His move brought him from West Sussex where
he headed a flourishing college department and served
part-time in a large parish church. His wife, Althea, a
psychologist, ran a counselling practice, and, with
their young son, they were settled, successful and
fulfilled.

For Brian, the move to Wells was an example of
the turmoil that can be associated with trying to find
out what God wants us to do with our lives. Brian's
journey shows how God is involved with the journey
of faith. It is a journey which shows how complicated
it can be to discover God's guidance. It raises
questions about the times when things do not become
clear until long after decisions are made and

implemented. It also shows how God does not force us into decisions against our will but leaves the way open for us to co-operate with him.

A Quest for Guidance

Even now, recalling the moment causes a slight shiver. I was seventeen, in the first term of my final year at secondary school, walking down the long upper corridor which would take me past the headmaster's study and on towards the science labs. It was a feeling of being trapped. It all sounds a trifle melodramatic nearly thirty years on, but it was symptomatic of a disturbing period of my life. My faith was real; God was with me – somewhere – and the current crisis was transitory, or so I hoped. And yet, as I walked past the classrooms a feeling of near panic came over me.

My forte was mathematics. Both the concepts and the practice of mathematics through to the sixth form had, generally, come easily. I had been fascinated by the logic and order of the subject and enjoyed the deep satisfaction of consistently attaining the 'right' answer. High marks and complimentary reports in the subject had become the norm. So it became increasingly apparent that Pearson B.W. of the Science VIth would 'read mathematics' – assuming he could squeeze a pass in another subject. But the awful truth was now before me. I wanted no more of mathematics. And the thought of three years of university-level maths gave me the shudders. Was I trapped? Was there another option?

I sought advice and the advice was 'read maths'. 'Then what?' I asked the careers officer. A pause, and then he suggested triumphantly, 'Accountancy'. Even pre-Monty Python I had an image of accountants which bore a close resemblance to Cleese & Co's portrayal – so no, thank you. My careers guru was not ready to admit defeat. 'Become a maths teacher,' he proclaimed. With an arrogance that befitted my late teens I wanted to tell him exactly what I thought of that, but my nature (polite and cowardly) ensured I held my peace. I turned to prayer.

God and I had been getting on pretty well of late. Since the age of three I had attended some group or organization attached to my parish church in south-east London. Sunday school, choir, youth club – I loved it all. In time I was given responsibility and enjoyed both organizing and participating. I also sat at the feet of no-nonsense preachers who taught me the fundamentals of faith from the Bible, and prepared me for my confirmation. The youth club did much to prepare me for a world where my Christian values would be challenged, tested and occasionally mocked. I was discovering faith as a practical part of my life as well as a set of statements of belief. I also faced the paradoxes of living out the Christian faith in the excitement of the liberated Sixties. I discovered what it meant to take risks in holding on to that which I believed to be right. God had given me a lot and I don't think I ever knowingly took it for granted – but neither do I recall asking a great deal of him. So perhaps crunch time was imminent, because I needed guidance. Advice from family and professionals was accessible but it was also predictable. I felt I needed to change direction, but

I longed for it to be a move towards, rather than away from, something.

As I did pray, my thoughts and prayers became intermingled – as I walked across Blackheath to the bus-stop, or climbed the hill from church to home, or filled in time while the physics master looked for a voltameter which still worked. My burden was becoming a distraction, and I increasingly invited God to share in that distraction.

One day I emerged from the unholy sanctuary of the prefects' room to head for the physics lab. At the same time the headmaster appeared from his study and walked towards me. He was looking past me but as he drew closer he greeted me warmly. I liked him a great deal. I became aware that he had stopped and was about to address me, even though he had passed me by several paces. 'Pearson, I've got something in my study I want you to read. It only arrived in today's post. I think it's for you.' I went to his room, he handed me a booklet, said there was no hurry to return it, and we continued our journeys to opposite ends of the building.

It was 1966 and the technological revolution was shifting up a gear. A few company names associated with the almost sci-fi world of computers were beginning to become commonplace. IBM was one of them, and I now clutched an application form for one of their sponsored studentships. My mind was no longer distracted. It had rarely been more focused and, as I read, I became exhilarated. I hardly understood a word – engineering jargon, early computer-speak, Americanisms – but I wasn't reading the words; I was being wooed by the images behind the words and the illustrations of electronic machinery.

A year later I was in student digs on the outskirts of Brighton and at a low ebb. Six months into my college-based computer training I remained thrilled by the technology but downhearted at the realization that this course required not only university-level mathematics but a similar level of statistical maths. I was struggling with these subjects and haunted by the prospect of failing to progress to the next stage, even though I was more than competent in the pure computing areas. I felt badly let down – though I wasn't sure who was to blame. Had I failed to read the small print? Was this all a terrible mistake? Had I misread God's guidance? That was tricky because God and I were not talking a great deal at that time. I think I had slipped out of the habit. I was far less aware of him in Sussex than in south-east London. I couldn't find him in church worship and struggled to engage with him in prayer and study. I had stumbled into the wilderness and again experienced a disturbing chill.

This time there was no miraculous intervention of a benign headmaster but rather a slow trudge by which, with the comfort and support of friends whom I grew increasingly to value, I emerged with sufficient strength and conviction to survive interim exams. Beyond that, though it was not plain sailing, each step forward brought confidence and a deeper sense of 'rightness' about what I was doing. Especially outside the lectures, I blossomed and found a variety of new skills.

After several years at the sharp end of the computer system supply and support industry, I decided to pass on my skills and experience in higher education. Not only was there a new generation to indoctrinate into the wonders of new technology, but there was a massive re-education and in-service training programme for mature students. The demand for courses at every level was insatiable with the arrival of the first Personal Computers and pioneering work with international computer networks; these were exciting times and I relished the privilege and the buzz of operating at the cutting edge.

By the mid-Seventies my professional interests were becoming more focused in the field of systems analysis. It was then that I was asked to supervise a research student who had previously been a male nurse in his native Hong Kong. Over a period of some months I visited a hospital intensive care unit to supervise his project. One of the nursing staff I met regularly I knew to be a Christian. She was an Irish Catholic with a rather curt manner with her colleagues and intruders, but most tender with the premature babies in her charge.

On one occasion I entered the 'overflow' ward which had served as our base, and found both incubators occupied. The babies were twin boys whose combined weight was less than 2kg. They were many weeks premature, very dark, quite still and almost swamped by wires, tubes and life-sustaining paraphernalia. There appeared to be precious little life in them – yet those lives were precious. I knew them to be precious to their parents, I sensed they were precious to the staff, I believed they were precious to God and, curiously, I felt they were precious to me. I visited next about two weeks later but found that only one of the incubators was occupied. The nurse was busy next door with some parents and then the phone needed answering so it was some time before I could ask her the question on my mind. 'What happened to Paul?' I was denied a straight answer for a while. Indeed I misread the evasiveness as an attempt to soften the impact of sad news. Then she admitted, 'He's with his mother in the main ward, and,', anticipating my next enquiry, 'his brother will join him next week.' I was elated, but she had not finished with me. 'And none of your fancy boxes nor their potions,' she said, nodding towards the office used by the doctors, 'would have made the slightest difference. TLC – tender, loving care – saved these little mites. And mind you remember that!' And I have remembered it.

On another day, when the emotions were not so strained and the ward was relatively quiet, we sat and talked over coffee. She was a wonderfully caring person with a deep faith. In addition to the requirements of her nursing duties she prayed for 'her babies'. She lived and breathed compassion for all living beings and this compassion was never more focused than when, on the ward with those mites who had arrived in this world far too early for their own good, she helped them in their struggle for survival. There I learned a lesson for life; never to let compassion become divorced from my work, even if that work primarily focused my energies on dumb machines and cold electronic logic. Guidance, I learned, is not just about the direction of the journey. It can bring us to a stop on the way, to teach, remind, refresh and reorientate before moving further along the same path.

Such experiences demonstrated that the two worlds of faith and work were not so distinct. The more I considered the connections and the blurred edges, the more I sensed a call to the priesthood. Those who knew me well were encouraging, and not altogether surprised, when I was recommended for training. Over the next three years I was exposed to a critical examination of the beliefs and doctrines which, I discovered, I had largely taken for granted.

My professional experience to date had equipped me to assess ideas and analyze processes, but it seemed odd to apply these approaches to my Christian faith. Following my ordination, I was intrigued to discover that my dual life could build bridges between the complementary worlds of faith and technology which I inhabited. So my new vocation, wherein the secular and sacred could be seen as one, provided me with opportunities to be a bridge-builder. Guidance, I pondered, was about personal vision as well as living in trust and obedience.

Statisticians say we move house, on average, every seven years. By that reckoning my wife, Althea, and I were overdue. And we felt it right that, if we were to move, it must be clearly towards something new rather than merely away from the familiar.

It was then that I had one of those occasional and extraordinary experiences when something seems to jump out of the page. I saw an advert for a lecturer-chaplain at an Anglican college. What an ideal combination, I thought. The two primary strands of my work experience combined in one job. The one negative element which nagged was the location. Most of our friends and relations lived around us in south London. Severing such close ties after thirty years would not be easy. It would also mean moving 350 miles north, and for a couple who had rarely ventured beyond Watford this was boldness indeed!

We spent four days away, of which two days were occupied with interviews and further briefings about the college, the job and the people. As the shortlist was further reduced I was one of the two survivors, and so Althea and I began even more intensive discussions about what it would be like to live so far from our roots. When the college principal called me in for the last time it was to tell me I was not being offered the job. He was charming, encouraging and most complimentary but as, later that day, Althea and I sat in our hotel bedroom taking stock, we asked God a question: What was all that about? The job looked just right, the location was attractive, the people pleasant and the interview panel positive. Yet I also knew the better man got the job. My beef was not with him nor the interviewers; it was with God. That may seem harsh but I was not so much disappointed as confused. In my naïvety I had assumed that God was guiding us, but now it felt as if we had been brought to the brink and then told to go away again. And then it dawned on us, and the truth as we now saw it made a great deal more sense. The issue before us was our willingness to move; to move away from the security of the familiar we had enjoyed over many years; to move into the markedly unfamiliar and to make a totally fresh start. It was a moment of stark realization that guidance and testing could be close companions. So were we prepared to upsticks unreservedly and move on?

From the hotel room I telephoned my parents with the news of the job. They informed me that a letter had arrived at my home from Worthing. It was inviting me for an interview for the post of head of a new department at a college. Six months later we had moved to Sussex, and the new chapter had begun.

For some ten years I had enjoyed short term chaplaincies, mainly in Switzerland, which for two or three weeks at a time placed me in a stunningly beautiful setting with responsibilities for English-speaking residents, tourists and casual workers. A church was put at my disposal, and if pastoral problems arose I was available to advise and support.

If anything, as the years passed, Althea's and my love of this work, the people and the country grew. It was no great surprise to find ourselves before an interview panel exploring an opening for a full-time chaplaincy based near Geneva. All seemed (again!) to go very well. But the organization's senior officer asked to meet us in our home. To our surprise he asked if we were prepared to put the current application on hold for the time being. There was another opening he would like explored. In fact, there were two parts to his approach. First he asked if I would don my management consultant's hat and visit a town in Switzerland for a few days, to see whether it could sustain a full-time chaplain. Second, if I concluded that it could, would I consider my suitability for it? This, I thought, could be an intriguing test of my integrity, given my current conviction that Switzerland was to be our new home and the undoubted enthusiasm of my new employer that I should join their team.

It was time to come clean with my family. Married for thirteen years, Althea and I now had an eighteen-month-old son. Only some of those married years had been childless by choice. We had experienced hopes dashed, disappointments and anguish that, at times, was both debilitating and depressing. We also knew that our wider family felt much of the pain that we had come to know. They were very supportive, very caring and understanding and so their endurance as much as ours was rewarded with the arrival of Thomas in October 1985.

So it was a difficult time as I thought about how to prepare my parents for a separation not only from Althea and me but from the long-awaited grandson they had only begun to get to know. True, according to an atlas Switzerland is not so far away; true, according to a calendar five years is not such a long time. But equally truly, an atlas and a calendar are not the yardsticks for measuring this sort of separation.

The courage I needed even to broach the subject eluded me until a day when I was driving my parents through Ashdown Forest. It was a hot day in early summer and I decided that a round of ice-creams was in order. I pulled off the road into a car park, and broke the news. Elsewhere, Althea was sharing our plans with her parents.

The few days in Switzerland were very testing. All manner of local business was spread before me and, to my embarrassment, I was already being publicly hailed as 'Their New Man'. It didn't help that it was an idyllic place to minister as a priest.

During the homeward flight I was already assembling my notes and attempting a first draft of my evaluation report. As was my style, I first drafted my conclusions. 'I see no justification for recommending the deployment of a full-time chaplain,' I read on my pad. One Swiss job down, one to go.

A second trip to Switzerland was arranged. I met with an incumbent priest and the local church leadership and then waited some days before a telephone conversation confirmed that this job was not the right one for me. Althea and I sat on the edge of the bed and repeated the question for God: What was that about? The trauma caused to our families and ourselves had all been unnecessary. We were not going abroad and our son would not be deprived of grandparental doting during his early years. We could terminate enquiries about trans-continental removals; we could suspend deliberations about retaining housing and other security in the UK; we could discard the sheaves of papers relating to health, education, employment and the rights (and lack of them) for foreign workers. What a complete and utter waste of time, energy and emotion, I complained.

I worked – and inwardly I seethed – for some further months. Having been unsettled with the anticipation of a move, it was proving difficult to settle again. In time I did, and it was then that my eye caught an advert in the church press for a research and communications officer attached to a bishop's office in the West country.

This didn't sound like me – so why did I keep re-reading the advert, and why did I show it to Althea? When the details arrived I noted against each line the degree to which my current CV matched. I rated myself somewhere between 65 and 75 per cent. Was that sufficient to warrant applying? I re-read the job spec. and my attention fixed on a single phrase. I was to discover later that it was the one phrase to have originated from my new employer – the rest having been drafted by his staff – 'I am looking for someone more willing to say "Why not?" than "Why?" ' I decided I wanted to work for someone who must have thought that way himself to welcome it in others.

At the same time God graciously answered my question. It was not so different from the last time. Was I prepared to abandon the familiar and the secure? Instead of directing me 600 miles east of Worthing, God placed me at a desk in a moated palace 150 miles to the west. I thought back to something in the Bible which had meant a lot to me since I had been ordained: 'Not that we are competent of ourselves to claim anything as coming from us; our competence is from God' (From Paul's second letter to the Corinthians).

Have I known guidance through my spiritual pilgrimage? Yes, I have, though I have found it to be an elusive thing. Whenever I thought it absent, it would suddenly appear. When I sought it or thought I detected it, it seemed to evaporate. Probably the best sightings I have had of guidance are those glimpsed as I have looked back over my shoulder. It must be so easy for God as he views my life's journey from a high vantage point. I know it is all so much clearer from above.

JOHN POLKINGHORNE

It is enormously helpful to have the insights of scientists who are Christians. John Polkinghorne's contribution to Christian thought, especially in the science-religion debate, has captured the attention and admiration of many from both disciplines.

John's journey has taken him both to the frontiers of research in cosmology and to those in need of pastoral support when he was a parish priest near Canterbury. Yet, as he writes, it becomes clear that in this there is no conflict. Many are grateful for John's remarkable ability to express complex ideas – be they of science or faith – in ways that the non-specialist can understand. For example, I like his illustration that music is more than vibrations in the air, even though this is all science says about it. For John, as well as the 'how?' questions of the scientist, there must also be the 'why?'

There is a balance in John's story. The discipline and order of mathematics and physics are reflected in his devotional life, with the pattern of Bible reading, psalms and prayer of the services of Morning and Evening Prayer. And worship centred on Communion is very important to John. I sense that it equips him to face the demands and rigours of his work.

I am also reminded by John that the academic world and the journey of faith are both involved in the search for truth. For John it is focused most especially in his passionate belief that all knowledge has its source in God.

From Physicist to Priest

People often think it's a bit odd that I am both a scientist and a Christian, a physicist and a priest. It seems quite natural to me because I believe I need the insights of both science and religion if I am truly to understand this rich and exciting world in which we live. If we're to get at the truth we need to answer both the how? questions which fascinate science, and the why? questions which are the concern of religion. To explain why I think that way I'll have to tell you a bit about my life.

I cannot remember a time when I was not a member of the community of the Church. I grew up in a Christian home and it was natural at an early age to accompany my parents to church. The worship in our Somerset village was not particularly geared to the needs of children but I was a well-behaved child, able to sit still when required. At some stage, I imagine when I was about eight, we acquired a rector who was a gifted preacher and I recall the way in which he could make incidents in the Bible come alive for his hearers. My parents did not give much in the way of explicit religious teaching at home but I absorbed through my pores the fact that religion was something of central importance in life.

This feeling for the centrality of faith continued through my later years at school (where, of course, I met bright young contemporaries who were contemptuous of religion), and through my national service in the army. I was a reasonably regular attender at our unit's chapel services, supported and encouraged by a fellow sergeant-instructor (who has subsequently become an archdeacon).

When I came up to Cambridge as an undergraduate in 1949, I encountered the Christian Union and was taken by someone to a freshers' sermon on the first Sunday of term. The preacher spoke of the call of Christ and of the need to respond. He used the story of Zacchaeus – an unpopular tax collector who wanted to see Jesus and was so short that he had to climb a tree to do so – as an illustration, emphasizing that at that time Jesus was passing through Jericho on the way to his death in Jerusalem, so that their encounter was a unique opportunity. I felt a strong call to respond and commit my life to Christ, and at the end of the service I was one of a long line of students who went forward.

At the time I would have described this as my 'conversion'. Looking back now I see that God has been continuously active in my life, and I would not say that there was a specific time when I was 'born again'. Yet the experience was certainly a significant one, marking a deepening of Christian commitment for me.

During my years at Cambridge as an undergraduate and research student, I was considerably involved in the activities of the Christian Union. I look back on those times with rather mixed feelings. There was a seriousness of personal commitment which was challenging and I have never lost the habit of the regular reading of the Bible which was encouraged. The Bible is very important to me in my own spiritual life but I read it now with a greater awareness of its strangeness, as well as its great spiritual strengths, than would have been the case then. As a clergyman I read through the psalms several times a year and I particularly value the honesty and great breadth of spiritual experience which is frankly recorded there. The psalmists are very bold, not afraid to say 'Wake up!' to God, if they think he's not paying enough attention.

And there were other things in the Christian Union life which I look back on with regret. There was a narrowness of vision and a certain fear of the richness of human life which I can see constrained me then, and from which it has taken many years for me to free myself completely. In that process I believe I have become a more open and honest Christian.

I have always been fascinated by the figure of Jesus Christ – his words of hope, his actions of compassion, his death and (I believe) his resurrection. Like so many down the centuries, I find that I cannot speak adequately about him without using the language of the divine as well as the language of humanity. No view of reality would make sense for me that did not have Jesus at its centre.

I am a very regular, organized sort of person and I think that helped me to keep going with Christian faith and practice during those years when marriage, a career and a young family imposed so many strains and demands on my time. I was also greatly helped by the fact that my wife, Ruth, is a person of deep Christian commitment and it has been a great joy for us to see our children grow up in the faith.

I am, of course, a scientist – which is sometimes seen as a problem for Christians. At no time have I felt I faced a crisis of choice between science and religion. I take very seriously all that modern science tells us about the structure and history of the universe. I also take very seriously the insights of the Christian faith into human status and destiny and the nature of God. I regard science and faith as being complementary, rather than conflicting. For me, it is both the Big Bang and God the Creator. Science by itself could never be enough. Science would simply describe music as vibrations in the air, but of course it is more than that. We need to ask not only *how* things happen, but also *why* things happen. Is there a meaning and a purpose behind what is going on in the world? There are, of course, puzzles about how the scientific and religious world views fit together. In recent years I have spent a good deal of time in thinking and writing about these issues, but I have never felt that I faced an either/or choice. For me it is very much 'both... and'. The rational beauty and order that science discovers in the physical world, and the fruitfulness of cosmic history – which has, in the course of fifteen billion years, turned an expanding ball of energy into the home of you and me – strongly suggest that there is a divine Mind and Purpose behind the world.

I spent somewhat more than twenty-five years working as a theoretical physicist, trying to use mathematics to understand the behaviour of the smallest bits of matter. I enjoyed my career in physics very much, not least in the many friendships I formed with students and colleagues. I regarded it as a Christian vocation to use my modest talents in that way. But I had long thought that I would not stay in theoretical physics all my life. The reason for that was that the subject was changing all the time, as new results and new ideas came along. As you grow older in these mathematically-based disciplines, you lose, to a certain extent, the flexibility of mind necessary to cope with incessant change. You have to run faster and faster to stand still, and after a while you get out of intellectual breath. I felt it would be best to quit the subject before it quit me. I wanted to leave while I was still a little bit ahead; before too many people were saying 'Poor old John, he's past it.' Approaching my fiftieth birthday, it seemed to me that the time had come. As I talked to Ruth about it – any change would have to be a joint decision – quite quickly and quite undramatically, we both reached the (somewhat surprising) conclusion that the right thing to do next would be to seek ordination.

Two experiences had helped me to that decision. About eight or so years before, a very interesting person had come to live near us with his family. Eric was a priest, had taught in Africa, and was now a qualified Jungian psychotherapist. He ran a fortnightly Bible study group which Ruth attended. After about a year, she said to me, 'You really ought to come too – something very important is going on here.' Slightly reluctantly, I agreed to set aside the time. The group was very diverse in age and experience. It tackled some pretty demanding books as background to the actual Bible study. Eric has great gifts as a teacher and inspirer, and over the seven years or so I attended the group, my eyes were opened to many new riches of Christian understanding and my faith was deepened. Belonging to that group was one of the formative experiences of my life.

The other significant event occurred one day when my vicar said to me, quite casually after a Sunday morning service, 'Have you ever thought of becoming a Reader?' (A Reader is a person in the Anglican church who is licensed to help with services, and who sometimes gives sermons.) I hadn't thought of that, but as I turned it over in my mind I felt interested in the possibility. Worship is very important to me in my own Christian life, and the idea of helping to lead it was very attractive. I am also a very pedagogic sort of person – I like telling people things and giving them explanations. Consequently, preaching was also an attractive possibility. So I said I would like to become a Reader and, in those informal days, I soon became one without having to go through the rather rigorous training which would nowadays be required.

In our city-centre church, with visiting preachers galore and academic clergymen in the congregation, there was not too much for a Reader to do, but I got experience by going out to little fenland churches and taking Evensong for them. I also began to do some hospital visiting, which I found demanding but rewarding. I learned that often there isn't much you can do for people in great distress but simply be with them, and also that that can itself be of some help.

All this prepared me for the decision to seek ordination. Although I enjoyed being a Reader, the

Eucharist – the service in which Christians obey Jesus' command to share bread and wine in memory of him – is central to my own spiritual life. I longed to be more involved.

It was then necessary to have my vocation tested by the ACCM (as it then was). I attended a selection conference, which was very encouraging and helpful. Wise people talked to me and I was grateful that they did not seem unduly impressed by my being a Cambridge professor (why should they? It was a very different kind of life I was now seeking to lead). It was a source of strength later, in training and early ministry, to know that my vocation had been assessed by people of maturity and experience.

Just before my forty-ninth birthday, I became a student again, at a theological college in Cambridge called Westcott House. It was quite an odd experience. I learned that, though it is easy to lecture for an hour, it is quite hard to listen to someone else lecturing for that length of time! I had many things to learn and I did the standard two-year 'geriatric' course (for mature ordinands over the age of thirty). My most important lesson at Westcott was to learn the value of saying the Daily Office, the unending cycle of Morning and Evening Prayer. As a priest I continue this, day in, day out, and I find that the cycle of prayer and praise, scripture and reading the psalms, forms a sustaining framework for my life.

When I was made a deacon in 1981, Ruth was having her own middle-aged adventure and had not yet completed her training to become an SRN. Consequently, we stayed in Cambridge for my deacon's year and I was a non-stipendiary (unpaid) curate at a church outside the city centre. I continued to teach for my college, though I had resigned my professorship on going to Westcott. When Ruth qualified and I was ordained as a priest, we went off for two years to a large working-class parish in South Bristol, where I was a full-time curate.

There is much about being a priest that you can only learn through apprenticeship, on the job. I was very fortunate that my first two vicars taught me a great deal in their very different ways. When I was licensed to go solo, so to speak, I went to be Vicar of Blean, a largish village just outside Canterbury. There, as in the previous two parishes, we found much friendship and encouragement. A lot of my time was spent knocking on doors, drinking cups of tea, just being with people. Sunday by Sunday I had the privilege of presiding at the Eucharist and preaching the gospel.

I had expected that the rest of my working life would be occupied in this way. However, just over two years later, I was offered, out of the blue, the opportunity to return to Cambridge as the Dean of Trinity Hall – a job which is essentially being the parish priest of this small and friendly college. After thought, prayer and a very helpful talk with the Bishop of Dover, I decided to accept.

In a way, it was an embarrassment to return to the academic world so soon. But I had come to the conclusion that part of my job would be to write about the relationship between science and religion. While at Blean, I had completed the manuscript of a book, but it was clearly going to be easier to continue this activity in the setting of a university, and in the end that persuaded me to return as a priest to where I had so long been working as a physicist.

Even more surprisingly, three years later came the invitation to become the President of Queens' College, Cambridge. Although you do not have to be a clergyman for the job, I have the opportunity to play my priestly part in its services.

My present life is privileged and pleasant. I have to confess, however, to a nostalgia for the parish work in which I spent a brief five years. I hope that when I retire I may be able to return to it in an honorary and part-time capacity. The life of the parish priest is one of great satisfaction. It may seem odd to say so, but I specially miss taking funerals. To be able to be with people in their times of sorrow (and sometimes anger) and to be able to speak of the Christian hope that death is not the end, is a great privilege. I can say that because I believe that God is faithful and never abandons us, and that he showed his faithfulness when he raised Jesus from the dead that first Easter day.

Since I went to Westcott, my life has been full of changes and surprises. I can see that God has been involved in the whole experience and I am grateful for it. When my decision to turn from physics to the priesthood became known there was a bit of comment in the press. This brought with it an unexpected bonus. One of the people who read the paragraphs was a nun who had attended my lectures at Cambridge some years before. She wrote to me and we began a correspondence. After a while it seemed a good idea to meet, and I visited her community in a convent near Monmouth. That was the start of a relationship with the Sisters of the Society of the Sacred Cross which has been of great importance to me in my spiritual pilgrimage.

Tymawr is my spiritual home and I try to visit there each year and make a short retreat. The existence of the enclosed religious orders is a powerful, largely hidden, prayerful presence in our society. I am continually astonished at the wide network of people who are in touch with the Sisters. When I was suddenly and seriously ill while a curate in Bristol, I was much sustained by the knowledge of the prayer of the Sisters at a time when God seemed very far away from me. I know that life in the cloister can be hard and that communities are not always as equable on the inside as they appear from the outside, but the peace that such communities provide for their visitors is a costly and precious gift, for which I and many others are very grateful.

Amid all the sharp changes that my life has brought me, I feel also a great degree of continuity. I have always been part of the worshipping and believing community, whether as layman or as priest. I have always been caught by the thrill of scientific discovery, whether as a professional physicist or as an interested spectator. Above all, although my life changed in all sorts of ways when I turned my collar round, there is the great continuity that, as physicist and as priest, my life has been concerned with the search for truth. I am a passionate believer in the unity of knowledge, that ultimately science and theology are in harmony, and I believe that unity finds its source and guarantee in the One God who is the Creator of this wonderful universe in which we live.

DONALD SOPER

A giant of Methodism, a great apologist of the Christian faith and a fearless preacher; Lord Soper has never been a man of half measures. Passion and energy remain the marks of his ministry. Donald is his own man – and has consistently confounded those who would pigeon-hole him.

The media has a habit of stereotyping people involved in the church, and so I admire 'maverick' characters who defy these expectations. Donald Soper, whether in the pulpit, on a soap box, or in the Upper Chamber of Parliament, always commands attention. He has in the past both surprised and shocked, and he has often spoken about things from which others shy away, or fail to present clearly.

My invitation to him to share something of his journey arose both from curiosity and admiration. I think he is one of this country's most significant church leaders, and his wisdom and insight come from a refusal to accept the status quo as unchallengeable. His story is inspirational because it is punctuated with sharp questioning, and shows his readiness to let doubt drive him to find credible answers.

I am sure he and I have not found identical answers to all the common questions we have explored, but I always admire Donald Soper the enquirer.

Discoveries
on the Way

I was to meet Lord Soper at the West London Mission. He had opted to be interviewed as a contributor to this volume, and this turned out to be an ideal way for him to share something of his journey.

Over the years, his writing has been both profound and, at times, provocative. His great strength is his spontaneity, wit and clear thinking. In fact, allowing Lord Soper to tell his story this way shows a man who makes Christianity attractive, relevant and authentic.

I entered a small sitting room. Lord Soper sat relaxed in an armchair, an old man whose eyes were bright and his mind razor sharp. There was also a hint of impishness. He was quick to put me at my ease so I invited him to begin his story. I confessed that I could not promise to use all of what he provided. 'Just write what interests you and might be helpful,' he said, to reassure me. And, no, he would not need to see my draft; 'I think I can trust you,' he added with a grin.

He spoke warmly of his home life, of caring parents and of church being central to family activities. Indeed, his earliest impressions were that of church being an extension of the home. His father was a Sunday school superintendent, where his mother also taught. But even in those days he sensed that his Christian background was rather narrow, though religion was an integral part of his normal life.

Going to Cambridge provided the jolt which made him think about his faith. This was a time of national restructuring following World War I. There was confusion in so many areas of life; a contrast to the perceived stability of home. New ideas abounded in Cambridge – what was true, what was right, what was reliable? I asked him to recall his feelings at the time. It was, he confessed, a deeply perplexing time when he had left behind the clear teaching of his upbringing. In its place was thinking which challenged so much of what he had thought to be solid.

'So what was your reaction?' I asked. 'I became an atheist,' he replied, in a rather matter-of-fact way. I asked what lay behind such a drastic decision. He indicated that he had not been at peace with himself, his faith or the confusion of ideas which were then rife. As he described his feelings at that time it seemed to me as if he was taking stock of a new world where many of his assumptions had been shattered. Yet shedding his faith did not come easily.

Soon after his arrival at Cambridge the young Soper had visited the local Methodist church and offered to help run the Sunday school. That, in the light of his background, seemed entirely natural. Yet, faced with such disillusionment with the Christian faith, he felt compelled to resign his position as a teacher. At the same time he admitted that he did not wish to abandon entirely his link with the Church. For him, even at that time, the Church remained important.

I asked him why he thought this might have been. He wasn't entirely sure, but maybe it was a hangover from his youth, perhaps the people – whom he liked – or his sense of responsibility for the youngsters in his care. Perhaps, he suggested, he enjoyed the responsibility and was loath to relinquish it. Certainly there was security to be found in the familiarity of the surroundings. It could even have been a reaction to a society where he saw the experience of change more evident than was the direction or objective of change. 'I have little doubt, though,' he added, 'that God had a hand in my holding on to that link.' The Church – and in particular the Methodist Church – remained an important spiritual resource and, though he ceased to teach the youngsters, he was proficient enough in playing the piano to accompany the Sunday school's worship.

I wondered how he now viewed this transition period in his spiritual life. His answer pointed to the need to shed his inherited faith and to discover what he himself believed. He described it as rather like the need to discover and furnish one's own home rather than remaining a lodger in the family residence, however comfortable and secure that may be. So if his faith was being formed, what were the key elements in this period of personal discovery?

His response identified two strands. Firstly, he discovered much of the reality of God in sacrament; for him it was rather like talking to God and this was a vital factor in mapping a journey. This 'conversation' brought with it a very clear consciousness of his own wrongdoing, together with the temptation to avoid or suppress that consciousness. Secondly, the formation of his faith was very closely allied to his education. Cambridge had demonstrated vividly just how much he had to learn; it also provided a unique environment within which to explore, analyze and assemble insights that enabled him to weigh the experiences of the past and present. I concluded that the formation of his faith depended on a steady progression of events rather than a sudden experience.

For many people, Lord Soper is best known for his open-air work. How, I wondered, had that come about? He told me that he first went to speak at Tower Hill in 1926. He was confronted with moral and intellectual issues that were all the more disturbing for someone claiming to be a Christian. What did it mean? In the end, rather than rejecting Christianity, he sought to reassess it, and that process of reassessment has remained an integral part of his spiritual journey ever since. He spoke of an inherent dissatisfaction which remains with him still, which stimulates him to enquire and explore Christianity and the world.

It was not long before he gained something of a reputation for his unique style of ministry. Once he was spotted while abroad. He had been travelling in Japan and the plane journey had been interrupted. The pilot had landed and all the passengers had been guided into a shed at one end of the airfield. Amidst the confusion and concern of those in the large crowd came a voice addressing him: 'This is a long way from Tower Hill, Mr Soper!' The man behind the voice told Soper of his experience of hearing him at Tower Hill and how it had challenged his own thinking. Although at the time Soper was fairly new to this type of work he resolved to give more time and attention to it and develop the particular skills he realized would be necessary to sustain it.

What techniques has he honed over the years to become such an effective communicator to the passing trade of enquirers and tourists? One of his most crucial guidelines was never to go beyond people's interest. He maintained that open-air speakers are at their most effective when they seize the opportunity to speak on something that engages the minds of their listeners. They are likely to cease being effective when their primary aim is to win an argument. I wondered therefore how far his speaking was designed to challenge; didn't he seek to see minds and hearts changed? He cautioned that it was dangerous to ask people for instant decisions. It was far better to build up relationships and rapport. But what about rapport with a heckler? I asked. That was unlikely to be fruitful. 'On the contrary,' he told me, 'I have seen many a heckler become a listener, and listeners can easily become enquirers.'

But what of the nuisance element of hecklers, with their attempts to distract the genuine listeners? Clearly, Lord Soper had plenty of experience to cope with them. Of course there were disturbed and angry people, who needed the attention the occasion offered because they had been denied it elsewhere. Some would have done well to bring their own soap-box but perhaps lacked the confidence or conviction to go solo. 'But,' Lord Soper added, 'I've been more than grateful to my hecklers on some occasions, such as when I was arrested.' This was when he was conducting a meeting at Tower Hill and the police intervened, on the grounds that

Soper was drawing a crowd too near to the Crown Jewels! In the light of this intrusion the hecklers switched allegiance and sided with the man they had been taunting, vainly attempting to defend him from the police. But whatever the reason, the continuation for so many years of open-air oratory, verbal jousting with hecklers and serious debate has caused thousands to pause or linger for a while close to an elderly but robust cleric at Hyde Park's Speaker's Corner.

Lord Soper then offered some back-handed advice for would-be open-air speakers. If it was numbers they were after then bring sex into the subject; that usually doubled the size of the gathering. However, it tended to halve the quality of the discussion.

I reminded him that some of his most profound statements were from his commitment to a Christian socialism; I wondered if he had become disillusioned with this, if perhaps he felt that socialism, as he had understood it, had now disappeared. His interpretation was that socialism had shifted to a point where it attempted to improve on capitalism which, for him, lost sight of some basic issues. Underlying his frustration and concern was the changing nature of language. He regretted the demise of verbal clarity and precision: words have come to mean whatever one wants them to mean. But meaning, he argued, comes from experience, and experience is always bigger than the word.

But what of more orthodox preaching, I wondered; what of the image of the Methodist minister powerfully proclaiming God's truths, armed with a large black Bible and an unswerving faith and conviction? Lord Soper's initial response took me by surprise. 'I see the Bible as one of the greatest hindrances to evangelism,' he said. 'It either says everything or nothing; you can't offer it as the answer to problems to those for whom it has no credibility.' And yet, Lord Soper was swift to add, the Bible remains the most precious document we have. I asked how *he* sought to present the gospel. He maintained that if you can present the humanity of Christ, his divinity will look after itself. Jesus can be revealed as the human photograph of God, and that is what so many people Lord Soper had met yearned to discover. Time and again he would see people finding no unknown deity but what they had been looking for. 'There, you see, the evangel becomes alive in the contexts of daily life.'

What of his continuing and deepening relationship with Jesus? He referred me back to the context of this collection of stories. We were talking about journeying where there is both a gamble and an assurance. There is no detailed map of the future or of our life's journey but the man Jesus offers himself to each of us as a guide. He will answer our questions and help us resolve difficulties as we travel into unfamiliar territory.

It sounded simplistic so I pressed the point, and Soper underlined the two characteristics of the journey which he had introduced: gamble and assurance. His experiences had presented him with complex dilemmas which he had sought to resolve through his relationship with Jesus. That relationship provided him with the assurance he needed, even if, from a distance his actions looked more like a gamble.

Our conversation moved to the subject of the Church and I enquired about his own view of the Church, from the standpoint of a Methodist minister. I was also interested in what he thought about and hoped for from the wider Church. His first comments were of a general nature. Church, for him, is an expression of our need to share. If we attempted to work alone we would achieve much less. For this reason he expressed regret that Anglicans and Methodists had missed an opportunity to unite. He hoped that the will to unite would not lost and that the means would be found. He felt that the breadth that was now to be found in Methodism demonstrated how both the proclamation of the gospel in preaching and the sacramental aspects of the worshipping community could be contained, just as the two were evident and valued within the Church of England.

As my conversation with Lord Soper drew to a close I reflected on what I had discovered about both the man and his ministry. Throughout his journey of faith, he had endeavoured to remain utterly faithful to his calling as a Methodist minister and preacher of the gospel. Whether on Tower Hill or at Hyde Park Corner, in a chapel pulpit or in the West London Mission, his proclamation of that gospel has consistently been fashioned by the social issues of the day. Yet the power and focus of his preaching has not wavered. His primary concern has always been for the kingdom of God. Social issues of the day – matters concerning the environment, pacifism – yes, he has addressed them all, but in ways which sought to point to the kingdom and to God's way, to Christ through whom God and his kingdom can be known.

SIR ARNOLD WOLFENDALE FRS 14TH ASTRONOMER ROYAL

*T*he debates which centre around science and religion often generate more heat than light. Generalizations and ill-founded assumptions abound, and frustration soon sets in. But we can hope that someone has a point of view that shows reason and common sense; at its very best it is the voice of someone who is highly regarded in both camps. Professor Arnold Wolfendale is such a person: until recently the Astronomer Royal, a renowned academic at Durham University and a Christian absorbed by the wonder of God's remarkable creation.

In my own journey I have tried to think about the 'both-and' option of the science and religion debate rather than accept as inevitable the 'either-or'. It is not always a popular line, especially as it can invite the cynic's accusation of compromise. Yet Arnold Wolfendale believes that the order which underpins the universe and science is of God. It is a conviction which affirms that there is an awe and wonder into which the scientist as much as any other of God's people can enter.

Professor Wolfendale issues an invitation to look

deeply into God's creation and to let both reason and revelation speak. Some of his conclusions and the models he uses to illustrate them challenge traditional ideas, but that is no reason to ignore them. A journey for anyone should change perspectives, and I am grateful for the viewpoint Arnold Wolfendale presents to fellow travellers.

The Evolution of the Universe and the Evolution of Belief

Notwithstanding the interest in religion shown by many scientists, including such eminent historical figures as Isaac Newton, the views of a scientist on religion are, in general, no more worthy of attention than the views of anyone else on this important subject. However, two aspects do command attention.

The oft-claimed antagonism between science and religion is one. The famed, though rarely rigorously practised, application of 'the scientific method' – logical testing of theories by experimental measurements of physical quantities producing repeatable results – by scientists to the problems of faith is another.

The duality of knowledge and experience

The modern physicist is much concerned with the problem that both matter and radiation can be described in two radically different ways. For example, under certain circumstances, radiation (such as visible light) is best considered as a series of waves; in other circumstances, viewing it as a collection of particles (called photons) gives a better understanding of its subsequent behaviour.

In astronomy, our knowledge of the universe comes to us both through radiation – in the form of light, X-rays, gamma rays, radio waves and so on – and in the form of matter – meteorites, tektites and cosmic ray particles. These two views are complementary and a full understanding of the cosmos needs both.

In my opinion, far from being antagonistic to faith, this science analogy has relevance to religion. Human behaviour can be thought of as having both physical and spiritual components and a full description of the place of mankind in the universe needs an appreciation of both.

The question of the planes

It is not uncommon to regard physical and spiritual aspects as occupying different dimensions of life. Of course such interpretations are fraught with pitfalls but they have value in helping people to 'grasp the ungraspable'.

An interesting development of this area has recently arisen by an unusual route. For a number of reasons I have suggested that the Church of England should have the equivalent of the Pontifical Academy of Sciences. I expounded my views in a letter to *The Times* (7 November 1992), when I wrote:

Sir, Your article and editorial on Galileo's rehabilitation by the Pope (October 31) and Brian Marsden's letter about Comet Swift-Tuttle on the same day present a fascinating juxtaposition which has relevance to what I see as a great need in our established church: the equivalent of Rome's Pontifical Academy of Sciences.

Whilst it is true that the Church of Rome has taken rather a long time to acknowledge its error in condemning Galileo for his support of the sun-centred planetary system, Rome takes a particular interest in the relationship between science and religion. The present Pope has been singularly anxious to initiate discussion on this weighty topic – and is to be congratulated for it.

Turning to our own Church – for which many of us have a great affection – there seems to be a near-vacuum in thinking about some of the great science/religion problems of the age. In my own subject, I would list attitude towards the origin of the universe (where absurd comments about seeing the 'face of God' in the ripples in the cosmic microwave background need reasoned comment), the search for life elsewhere in the universe, the possibility of cometary impact (Swift-Tuttle is the latest candidate) and so on.

It is not good enough to compartmentalise science and religion and say that there is no overlap: in all my examples it is considerable. The established Church (and others too?) could through a 'Canterbury Science Academy', provide a forum for reasoned debate on these and other issues.

If the Church were to occupy a leading role in analysing and providing advice, instead of merely tagging along behind, it would send out a forward-looking message to all, not least the fascinated young; such a move might even help to arrest its decline.

My view, still firmly held, is that more young people will be attracted to the Church only if it grasps the nettle of scientific enquiry and is in the van, rather than the rear, in studying some of the weighty matters referred to in my letter. Many religious organizations do indeed take an interest in science but I feel that a higher profile is needed.

One interesting issue to arise from all this is the dichotomy of science and religion in terms of one relating to a line in one direction and the other to a line in the other, at right angles to the first. There is, however, a somewhat more sophisticated approach. I suggest that we consider the physical world as occupying a horizontal *plane* – all the physical laws and descriptions of the universe relate to this plane, and the alternative views of matter and radiation, and such like, also relate to this one plane. The spiritual plane on the other hand is at right angles to the material plane. But we can see that there is a profound difference – through any point there is only one horizontal plane, whereas there is in fact not one but an infinite number of vertical planes. This analogy can be pressed further by arguing that the various great religions of the world can be regarded as occupying different planes and the different shades of religious belief and practice within one faith ('high' church, 'low' church and so on) can be thought of as belonging to planes only a degree or two apart. There is no limit to it!

Many will say that this idea is not meaningful and of course there is no question of any literal significance to it, but if science and religion relate to different aspects of human endeavour then the idea may have some value.

What is certain, to me at any rate, is that the great religions of the world represent the results of efforts to explain the reason for our existence, and despite belonging to only one religion I would be the first to admit that the others have their own distinctive merits.

The Evolution of Belief

There are those who ask: 'Why do you, as a scientist, schooled in the area of hard fact, cause and effect, quantitative proof... go along with this religious business, with its lack of everything that the scientific method demands?' My answer has many parts, evaluating the dimension of religion which complements the scientific dimension rather than rivalling it. 'Secular' components include the value of religion as a way of life, as establishing a code of values and of personal attitudes. There is nothing new in this and, of course, humanists would claim that this area is catered for by their code; nevertheless, it represents an important dimension.

Another component relates to the beauty represented by church architecture (which reaches near perfection in my own church: Durham Cathedral) and church music. Although apparently secular in nature, the way of life, the buildings and the music do add up to something more than the sum of the parts, particularly when tradition and an appreciation of the many centuries of continued worship in many of our churches is included. Hopefully, one's spiritual beliefs evolve and strengthen as time progresses and as one becomes more and more sensitive to the ethos present at one's place of worship.

Mention of 'evolution' brings me to the evolution of 'Christianity' which I see in the Church. Many scholars now appreciate that many biblical 'happenings' were not, in fact, literally true; rather, that they were written as parables or illustrations. Many Christians are not willing to give way on 'miraculous' happenings, but to me this scepticism of the scholars is to be applauded. I feel that the underlying faith of the church does not need the many 'extras' with which we are presented in the Bible.

I believe that there is a core of belief that a Christian needs. My own specification of the core is a belief in the uniqueness of Christ as a teacher and, indeed, the 'Son of God'. The manner in which he appeared (the virgin birth) I do not understand – but appear he did. The messages he conveyed, by way of parables and actions, claimed by others as 'miracles', are also part of my core.

The Evolution of the Universe

There are some thorny problems for astrophysics in the origin and evolution of the universe. There seems little doubt that a 'Big Bang' occurred some 13 billion years ago and that the universe has been evolving ever since. But what preceded the Big Bang, and how will the universe develop in the future? Will the universe cease to expand eventually and then start to contract again, resulting in a 'Big Crunch'?! If so, will it bounce, and start off again? Indeed, is this the best way of understanding the origin problem, to say that there was no origin, and that the universe has always been expanding and contracting in turn? What about the nature of time – does it always proceed smoothly in the same direction or, if and when the universe starts to collapse, does time reverse along with space? What happens in black holes? Does passage through a black hole lead into another universe?

If one of the possible models of the universe is correct – in which it started from zero total energy, the potential energy being equal and opposite to the kinetic energy – then new universes may be generated. Where are they? How might they be recognized?

All the problems listed above have, in my view, a religious component. Concerning the nature of a God responsible for all things, my own faith has strengthened with increased experience of the discoveries of science; it is, to me, unthinkable that the whole edifice has a purely mechanistic origin. But there is a problem with God's revelation: here some rather obvious problems surface. Is Christ's appearance to be regarded as unique and confined to the present epoch? Two thousand years is a negligible time in comparison with the age of the universe. Have there been previous appearances? The near inevitability of life elsewhere in the universe, in my view, leads to obvious questions about the role of revelation in those places.

These questions are not put forward in a spirit of antagonism but rather to point up the rather primitive state of human knowledge at present in these areas. They indicate the need for more thought, as well as more scientific investigation, and the need to continue the evolution of religious belief. Such evolution need not destroy the basic tenets of Christianity but, as I have remarked already, tsome of the simplistic appendages of faith may need removal.

In earlier sections I have referred to the helpful imagery that can be used to circumvent the apparent antagonism of science and religion. A particular example from my own recent experience relates to a lecture that I gave in Durham Cathedral in May 1993, as part of the 900th anniversary celebrations. The main thrust of the lecture, entitled 'The Cathedral and the Cosmos', was to trace the development of our ideas of the cosmos over the life span of the cathedral by reference, in part, to those associated with the cathedral. I described the work of Bede, Thomas Wright, Van Mildert, Chevallier, and others, all illustrating in one way or another the thesis taken from Psalm 19 that 'The heavens declare the glory of God'. My final picture illustrated the cathedral's great Rose Window, which represents in a simple way cosmic science and Christian faith.

The window itself has evolved; starting from a smaller oriel in the thirteenth century it has been enlarged and improved, to reach its present, most impressive form, in the

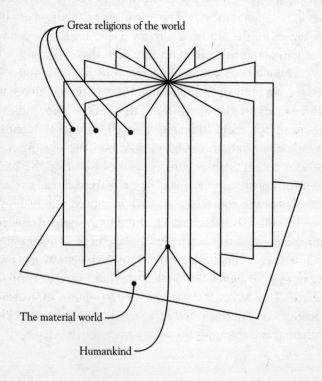

Great religions of the world

The material world

Humankind

eighteenth century. As an astrophysicist I see the whole representing the evolution of the material universe – 'how' things came about. Thus, the outer ring corresponds to the universe as it was some 300,000 years after the Big Bang, when the first atoms formed. It is from this period that the so-called cosmic microwave radiation came (at 2.7 degrees Kelvin); its small, so-called ripples, which were discovered in 1992 by the American satellite COBE.

Moving inward to the next circle we go back in time to when the universe was a few minutes old and the majority of the hydrogen and helium atomic nuclei were forming. Finally we arrive at the innermost circle which, in my analogy, corresponds to the unbelievably short time of 10^{-43} seconds after the Big Bang.

Now we have quite a passable theory of how the universe evolved for times subsequent to 10^{-43} seconds after the Big Bang but before that there are all sorts of problems, to do with how gravity behaved, what – if anything – came before the Big Bang and so on. Despite the present lack of knowledge about this region, my belief is that our knowledge will continue to evolve and that eventually we will have a good theory embracing the whole period.

All the above relates to *how* the universe formed and has evolved. To turn to *why* the universe behaved in the way it did – and *why* we are here to observe it – to me, the answer is bound up with the figure portrayed at the centre of the window – the figure of Christ. The details of 'why', like the details of 'how', may take a long time to come – in the event the 'how' question will certainly be easier to solve – but both deserve our continuing attention.